THE CATHOLIC UNIVERSITY OF AMERICA
CANON LAW STUDIES
NO. 240

ADMINISTRATIVE RECOURSE

A COMMENTARY
WITH
HISTORICAL NOTES

BY

JUSTIN D. MCCLUNN, A.B., S.T.L., J.C.L.
Priest of the Diocese of Richmond

A DISSERTATION

Submitted to the Faculty of the School of Canon Law of the Catholic University of America in Partial Fulfillment of the Requirements for the Degree of Doctor of Canon Law.

THE CATHOLIC UNIVERSITY OF AMERICA PRESS
WASHINGTON, D. C.
1946

NIHIL OBSTAT:

H. LUDOVICUS MOTRY, S.T.D., J.C.D.
Censor Deputatus
Washingtonii, die 14 iunii 1946.

IMPRIMATUR:

+ PETRUS L. IRETON, D.D.
Episcopus Richmondiensis
Richmondiae, die 18 iunii 1946

Printed by
Graphic Arts Press, Inc.
Washington, D. C.

TO MY MOTHER
and to the memory of
MY FATHER

FOREWORD

The aim of this dissertation is to give a detailed study of administrative recourse, the remedy for injuries suffered from the use of the legislative, executive and coactive powers of ordinaries, and from the use of the dominative powers of superiors.

The Code of Canon Law allows the remedy of recourse to be used even when injuries have been suffered from the decrees of judges and from elections. To include a comprehensive treatment of these types of recourse in this dissertation would make it cumbersome and confusing, since they do not always follow the same norms as does administrative recourse. Consequently, it was decided to confine the subject of this dissertation to administrative recourse, and to consider recourses from judicial decrees and from elections in an incidental way only.

No detailed historical conspectus will be given, since recourse, as it is now known, is practically a new canonical institution. However, enough historical background will be furnished for comparing past and present remedies, and for noting their similarities and dissimilarities.

There has been, to this writer's knowledge, no detailed study published on this important canonical institute. Some lengthy treatises have dealt with recourse as mentioned in the Third Part of the Fourth Book of the Code, but none has considered recourse in general. General commentaries on the Code give little or no treatment of the nature, process and effects of recourse, except in regard to the administrative processes of the Fourth Book. Authors study in detail the nature, the process and the effect of judicial appeal, but they give little attention to appeal's administrative counterpart, recourse.

The writer wishes to take this occasion to express his sincere gratitude to the Most Reverend Peter L. Ireton, D.D., Bishop of Richmond, for the opportunity to pursue advanced studies in Canon Law; to the Faculty of the School of Canon Law at the Catholic University of America, Washington, D. C., for their kind guidance and assistance; and to all others who have aided in any way in the preparation of this work.

TABLE OF CONTENTS

CHAPTER V

THE SUPERIOR *AD QUEM*

CHAPTER VI

THE EFFECTS OF RECOURSE

CHAPTER I

REMEDIES AGAINST EXTRAJUDICIAL ACTS

A. *Pre-Code Remedies*

Under the pre-Code discipline there were two remedies against the administrative acts of superiors which allegedly injured the rights of subjects. Against such acts a subject could address a supplication, or he could make an extrajudicial appeal.

The ordinary remedy was the extrajudicial appeal.

To the ancient canonists appeal, in general, meant *cuiuslibet molestiae ad maiorem potestatem proclamatio*[1] or, as Bernardus Papiensis (†1216) defined it, "*sententiae vel gravaminis relevatio per proclamationem ad maiorem iudicem factam.*"[2]

For them and for all canonists, until the publication of the Code, appeal could be either judicial or extrajudicial. Judicial appeals were concerned with judicial acts. It was the remedy for injuries suffered in actions, sentences and all other judicial matters.[3]

Extrajudicial appeal, on the other hand, was concerned with matters that took place outside judgments.[4] It was the

[1] Rufinus, *Summa Decretorum* (ed. H. Singer, Paderborn, 1902), Causa II, quest. 6—hereinafter cited as Rufinus. Rufinus (*loc. cit.*) also furnished a more special definition: "Est igitur appellatio protestatio, sententiae iniquae vel suspectae querelam continens". This evidently referred to judicial appeal.

[2] *Summa Decretalium* (ed. E. A. Th. Laspeyres, Ratisbonae, 1860), Lib. II, tit. 20, § 1—hereinafter cited as Papiensis.

[3] "Appellatio est provocatio iniquae sententiae querelam continens" —*Glossa Ordinaria* s. v. *liceat* in c. I, C. II, q. 6; cf. also Rufinus' more special definition given in the footnote above; ". . . (appellatio) judicialis est, quae interponitur ab actibus judicialibus, sive de iis quae in judicium veniunt, et circa istud accidunt"—Schmalzgrueber, *Ius Ecclesiasticum Universum* (5 vols. in 12, Romae, 1843-1845), Lib. II, tit. 28, n. 5—hereinafter cited as Schmalzgrueber.

[4] ". . . appellatio fit in iudicio, provocatio vero extra iudicium"—Cardinalis Hostiensis (Henricus de Segusio), *Commentaria in Quinque Decretalium Libros* (5 vols. in 3, Venetiis, 1581), Lib. II, tit. *de appellationibus*, cap. 50, n. 12—hereinafter cited as Hostiensis; Panormitanus (Nicolaus de Tudeschis), *Commentaria in Quinque Libros Decretalium*

remedy to be used in cases concerning elections, postulations, acts of filling ecclesiastical offices, canonical monitions and injunctions, the visitation of dioceses and of religious houses, the appointment of tutors and curators, the extrajudicial acts of superiors and ordinaries, etc. The list of matters in which one could appeal extrajudicially was almost limitless, since it covered every kind of extrajudicial injury already suffered, or even merely threatened or feared.[5]

Pope Alexander III (1159-1181) pointed out that extrajudicial appeals were more appropriately designated as summons or citations to start a cause (*provocationes ad causam*),[6] since prior to the appeal there was no process, for it was only with the appeal that the case began.

In their considerations on appeal pre-Code canonists grouped extrajudicial and judicial appeal under the one category, and they treated extrajudicial appeal as merely a slight variation from judicial appeal. When they defined appeal, they made their definition wide enough to include *provocationes ad causam.*[7]

Moreover, the *Decretum Gratiani,*[8] which appeared about the year 1140 and the authentically promulgated Decretal Col-

(5 vols. in 8, Venetiis, 1588), tit. *de appellationibus, recusationibus, et relationibus*, (II, 51, 7)—hereinafter cited as Panormitanus; "Appellatio extrajudicialis fit ab actibus, vel decretis extrajudicialibus, quibus aliquis gravatur"—Schmalzgrueber, Lib. II, tit. 28, n. 4.

[5] Cf. c. 51, X, *de appellationibus, recusationibus et relationibus*, II, 28.

[6] "Si vero a gravamine et ante litis ingressum fuerit appellatum, huiusmodi audietur appellans, quoniam sacri canones etiam extra iudicium passim appellare permittunt: nec solent huiusmodi dici appellationes, sed provocationes ad causam."—c. 5, X, *de appellationibus, recusationibus, et relationibus*, II, 28.

[7] E.g., the general definition of Bernardus Papiensis (footnote 2 of this chapter), in which through the inclusion of the generic word "*gravaminis*" he showed that the use of appeal was not limited to the cases of judicial sentences, but was warranted also whenever some burden or injury was thought to occasion an unjust oppression. "Appellatio communiter definitur, quod fit a minore, seu inferiore, ratione gravaminis illati, vel inferendi, ad majorem, seu Superiorem, tanquam Judicem, facta provocatio."—Pirhing, *Ius Canonicum*, (5 vols. in 4, Dilingae, 1722), Lib. II, tit. 28, n. 1—hereinafter cited as Pirhing.

[8] C. II, q. 6.

lections of the thirteenth and early fourteenth centuries[9] grouped the laws on extrajudicial appeal with those on judicial appeal.

However, even the ancient canonists recognized that there were many points of difference between judicial and extrajudicial appeal. Hostiensis (†1271)[10] noted some seventeen differences between the two kinds of appeal, and Panormitanus (1386-1453)[11] mentioned fourteen differences. But many of these differences were quite minute, and one may duly conclude that some of the delineated differentiations were stressed as a result of the special predilection that medieval scholars had for marking distinctions.

Later canonists[12] listed three main differences between judicial and extrajudicial appeal:

1) A judicial appeal was an appeal in the strict sense of the word.[13] An extrajudicial appeal, on the other hand, was an appeal in a less distinctive sense of that term, since there was not involved the need of any properly judicial action in the rehearing of the case.
2) A judicial appeal was always interposed against the final sentence of a judge, and presupposed the presence of an allegedly sustained injury. An extrajudicial appeal, however, was employed against the decree issued by a superior, or against the direction imposed by some other party;[14] not only when the aggrieved

[9] X, *de appellationibus, recusationibus, et relationibus*, II, 28; *de appellationibus*, II, 15 in VI°; *de appellationibus*, II, 12 in Clem.

[10] *Op. cit.*, Lib II, tit. *de appellationibus*, cap. 50, nn. 10-12.

[11] *Op. cit., de appellationibus, recusationibus, et relationibus*, (II, 51, 7-15).

[12] Reiffenstuel, *Ius Canonicum Universum* (5 vols. in 7, Parisiis, 1864-1870), Lib. II, tit. 28, n. 11—hereinafter cited as Reiffenstuel; Schmalzgrueber, Lib. II, tit. 28, n. 5; Ferraris, *Prompta Bibliotheca, Canonica, Iuridica, Moralis, Theologica, necnon Ascetica, Polemica, Rubristica* (9 vols., Romae, 1885-1899), I, 292—hereinafter cited as *Bibliotheca;* Theodorus a Ried-Brig, *Manuale Practicum Juris Disciplinaris et Criminalis Regularium ad Usum F. Min. Cap.* (Romae, 1902), n. 211.

[13] Pirhing, Lib. II, tit. 28, n. 3.

[14] It was also possible to appeal extrajudicially against certain acts decided by a judge, for example, his appointment of tutors and guardians—cf. Pirhing, Lib. II, tit. 28, n. 3—inasmuch as such an act had

person thought his injury to be real, but also when he feared it as an impending evil.[15]

3) A judicial appeal generally operated with a suspensive effect, and any acts which were executed in the face of the pending appeal were invalid, so that they were to be declared as revoked in view of the irregular and outlawed procedure (*per viam attentati*). An extrajudicial appeal, as a general rule, did not suspend the execution of the matter with which the appeal was concerned.[16] Yet, anything which was done directly contrary to the appeal as such could be revoked by the authority who received the appeal.[17]

The word *"supplicatio"* was used in three senses by pre-Code canonists. In the broadest sense it was used in designation of any petition addressed to someone in authority and requesting either the administration of justice or the granting of a favor.[18] Thus canonical writers spoke of a "supplication"

evidently been executed by him apart from the use of strictly judicial power.

[15] C. 51, X, *de appellationibus, recusationibus, et relationibus,* II, 28.

[16] Panormitanus, tit. *de appellationibus, recusationibus, et relationibus,* (II, 51, 10); Reiffenstuel, Lib. II, tit. 28, n. 10; Schmalzgrueber, Lib. II, tit. 28, n. 5; Verani, *Iuris Canonici Universi Commentarius Paratitlaris* (5 vols., Monachii, 1703-1708), Lib. II, tit. 28, n. 8; Ferraris, *Bibliotheca,* I, 292; Lancelottus, *Institutiones Iuris Canonici quibus Ius Pontificium singulari methodo libris quatuor comprehenditur* (Lugduni, 1779), 172—hereinafter cited as *Lancellotus;* Santi, *Praelectiones Juris Canonici juxta Ordinem Decretalium Gregorii* IX (2 vols., Ratisbonae, 1886), I, 239—hereinafter cited as Santi; Wernz, *Ius Decretalium* (2. ed., 6 vols. in 10: Romae, 1906-1913), V, 528, footnote.

[17] ". . . in provocatione cassantur illa tantum quae contra provocationem legitimam sunt facta"—Hostiensis, tit. *de appellationibus,* cap. 50, § 12; ". . . non ita invalida sunt gesta, pendente appellatione extrajudiciali nisi forte ipsi appellationi repugnent"—Schmalzgrueber, Lib. II, tit. 28, n. 125; "Extraiudicialis (appellatio) autem non suspendit exsecutionem, nec facit in contrarium attentata revocari, nisi sit bene et rationabiliter proposita, expressa etiam causa legitima appellandi, quae ut talis a superiore admissa . . ."—Ferraris, *Bibliotheca;* cf. also Durandus (Durantis), *Speculum Iuris* (Venetiis, 1577), Lib. II, partic. 3, § 11, n. 11, and Verani, Lib. II, tit. 28, n. 8.

[18] ". . . pro quibuscumque precibus judici porrectis sive ad justitiam sive ad gratiam impetrandam"—Schmalzgrueber, Lib. II, tit. 28, n. 2.

for a dispensation from an impediment to marriage. In another sense the term was used in designation of a request for a restitution of a previous juridical status (*restitutio in integrum*) namely, when there was alleged some probable cause other than the injury itself in consequence of which the judge was *ex officio* to come to the assistance of the injured party. Such a cause, for example, could be occasioned by the youth of the party, his absence or his probable ignorance.[19] Finally, in a restricted sense, the word "supplication" was used in designation of a petition submitted to a person in ruling authority, in order to obtain through his equity and kindness the petitioner's relief from the burden of a sentence against which there was no ordinary means of redress, namely by way of appeal, either judicial or extrajudicial.[20] The present study's interest in the term "supplication" centers in this restricted sense. Accordingly, whenever in this present study this term is mentioned without some further particular qualification, it is to be understood in this restricted sense.

It was stressed by canonical writers that for the reception of a favorable hearing this supplication was submitted with reliance on the equity and kindness (*quaedam benignitas*) of the ruling authority. This did not imply that there was no justice on the side of the petitioner; nor did it imply that, if the ruling authority decided against the sentence and in favor of the petitioner, his act was merely one of kindness. When canonists stressed the element of benignity they had in mind the fact that all the usual means of redress had already been used without success before the supplication was made, and that the sovereign's kindness allowed this one last effort to obtain relief from the alleged injustice or injury.[21]

[19] Cf. Pirhing, Lib. II, tit. 28, n. 6.

[20] "Supplicatio proprie dicta, et quantum ad propositum, est quaedam precum porrectio facta principi, ut is ex quadam benignitate restituat supplicantem adversus sententiam, contra quam non competit medium ordinarium"—Reiffenstuel, Lib. II, tit. 28, n. 18; Schmalzgrueber, Lib. II, tit. 28, n. 2; Pirhing, Lib. II, tit. 28, n. 6.

[21] ". . . allegata laesione, sive gravamine, petitur, ut sententia lata contra supplicantem retractetur, ex mera gratia et benignitate Principis; quia ordinarium appellationis remedium contra illum non competit . . ."—Pirhing, Lib. II, tit. 28, n. 6; cf. Reiffenstuel, Lib. II, tit. 28, n. 20.

Both justice and equity could be on the side of the petitioner, but the legal presumption did not favor his claim whenever the law forbade the use of an appeal, or when the petitioner had already employed the appellate procedure and the decision still stood against him in the sentence or the decree. Thereupon, when he had no further means of redress at his command, the kindness of the sovereign allowed one more hearing of the case.

The supplication amounted to a request for a review of the acts of the case with a hoped for revision of the import of the earlier sentence or decree.[22] However, while the usual review of the acts of a case (*revisio actorum*) in consequence of a judicial appeal held the execution of the sentence in abeyance, the supplication when admitted for a hearing did not operate with a similar suspensive effect.[23]

A Gloss on one of the Gregorian Decretals[24] pointed to two differences between appeal and supplication:

1) In general, an appeal entailed a suspensive effect, and consequently a sentence was not to be executed while an appeal from it was pending. However, while a supplication was pending, the sentence could be executed.[25]
2) A person who contemplated making an appeal was granted a period of ten days in which to do so, but a person who desired to submit a supplication for relief from what had been imposed on him by a sentence was accorded the right of exercising his option for a duration of two years.[26]

Authors pointed to still other differences.

[22] Pirhing, Lib. II, tit. 28, n. 8; Reiffenstuel, Lib. II, tit. 28, n. 18.

[23] Pirhing, *loc. cit.*

[24] *Glossa Ordinaria* s. v. *supplicavit* in c. 4, X, *de in integrum restitutione*, I, 41.

[25] This provision of the non-suspensive effect of supplication was based on the Roman Law of the Emperor Justinian (527-565): ". . . iubemus executionem causae sine fideiussione procedere, retractationis iure servanda illi qui se gravatum putaverit"—N. (119. 5).

[26] C. (7. 42) 1.

1) An appeal was carried to an authority higher than the one against which it originated. Thus an appeal had to pass from a diocesan court to the metropolitan court. A supplication, however, could be addressed to the same sovereign who had pronounced the previous sentence or issued the earlier decree.[27]
2) Appeal was the ordinary remedy; supplication was the extraordinary one. The latter was allowed to be used only when the ordinary remedy was no longer available.[28]
3) An appeal for redress against an injury could be invoked even while the legal suit (*lis*) was pending; but a supplication could usually be submitted only after a definitive sentence.[29]
4) One could appeal twice from the same definitive sentence, but one could only for a single time avail himself of the use of a supplication in the same case or issue.[30]

Since a supplication, by its very nature, was addressed to the ruling sovereign, the only proper authority in the Church to receive it was the Roman Pontiff.[31] The Pope alone had the authority to rescind or to cancel the effects of a sentence that had become a closed judicial issue (*res iudicata*). Occasionally canonists spoke of the possibility of submitting a supplication to the metropolitan, but they then used the term in a wider and more flexible sense.[32]

In its essential constitution a supplication was of an informal character. Hence in its form it did not have to comply

[27] Schmalzgrueber, Lib. II, tit. 28, n. 5; Pirhing, Lib. II, tit. 28, n. 7.

[28] Schmalzgrueber, *loc. cit.;* Reiffenstuel, Lib. II, tit. 28, n. 22; Pirhing, *loc. cit.;* De Camillis, *Institutiones Iuris Canonici* (3 vols., Parisiis, 1868), III, 137—hereinafter cited as De Camillis; Wernz, *Ius Decretalium,* V, n. 688.

[29] Schmalzgrueber, *loc. cit.;* Pirhing, *loc. cit.*

[30] Schmalzgrueber, *loc. cit.;* Pirhing, *loc. cit.;* De Camillus, *loc. cit.;* Wernz, *Ius Decretalium, loc. cit.*

[31] Pirhing, Lib. II, tit. 28, n. 6; Fermosinus, *Opera Omnia Canonica, Civilia et Criminalia* (2 ed., 14 vols.: Coloniae Allobrogum, 1741), III (*De Officiis et Sacris Ecclesiae*), 626—hereinafter cited as Fermosinus.

[32] Cf. Pirhing, Lib. II, tit. 28, n. 6.

with the many formalities which surrounded an appeal. Because of its informality and in view of its nature as a matter of gracious favor when the presentation rewarded the hopes of the petitioner, supplication was not the subject of many regulations in the early period of Church law. However, the fundamental principle that all Christians had the right to call on the Pope, as the Sovereign of the Church, for relief and help in any circumstance was expressed in several pseudo-Isidorian texts, which Gratian († ca. 1160) incorporated in his *Decretum* (ca. 1140).[33]

This fundamental principle was recognized in practice from the earliest years of the Church. Briccius († 443), the successor of St. Martin (316-397) as Bishop of Tours, some years after he had been driven from his see petitioned the Roman Pontiff for justice; the Pope reinstated him in his bishopric, and the people accepted the Papal decision.[34] Similarly, in 374 Peter, after his expulsion from the see of Alexandria by the Arians, called upon Pope Damasus (366-384) for help. Damasus reinstated him and excommunicated the usurper, Apollinaris, and his followers.[35] Felix of Epirus appealed to Pope Celestine I (422-432) against the threat of condemnation by a provincial synod, and the Pontiff intervened in favor of the appellant.[36]

Generally, pre-Code canonists looked to Roman Law for the norms which regulated supplications.

Usually when one supplicated a sovereign, the powers of the lesser judge were in no way impeded,[37] since the favorable

[33] E.g., cc. 4, 5, 6, 8, C. II, q. 6; Jaffé, *Regesta Romanorum Pontificum ab condita Ecclesia ad annum post Christum natum MCXCVIII*, 2. ed. correctam et auctam auspiciis G. Wattenbach, curaverunt S. Löwenfeld, F. Kaltenbrunner, P. Ewald (2 vols., Lipsiae, 1885-1888), nn. 183, 299, 323, 80—hereinafter cited as Jaffé.

[34] Gregory of Tours, *Historia Francorum*, Lib. II, Prologus; Migne, *Patrologiae Cursus Completus, Series Latina* (221 vols., Parisiis, 1844-1864), LXXI, 188—hereinafter cited as MPL.

[35] III Roman Synod of Damasus (374); Mansi, *Sacrorum Conciliorum Nova et Amplissima Collectio* (53 vols. in 60, Parisiis, 1901-1927), III, 485—hereinafter cited as Mansi.

[36] Celestine I, Epistola III—MPL, L, 427.

[37] C. 30, C. II, q. 6; C (49. 5) 4.

outcome which attended the presentation of a supplication was simply a concession that flowed from the sovereign's benignity. It was permissible for a person to make his supplication through a proxy.[38] Finally, one could supplicate only once regarding one and the same issue.[39]

It seems that it was in the early seventeenth century that canonists began to supplant the term "*supplicatio*" with the phrase "*recursus ad Principem*," indicating that outside of court procedure the redress which was sought at the hands of the sovereign ruler was in reality a "recourse with him."[40] However, the canonists' use of the term "*recursus*" was by no means consistent and uniform. Lega (1860-1935) listed four different meanings of the term:[41]

1) an extrajudicial appeal which lacked a suspensive effect;
2) a plea or entreaty presented to the Holy See in such cases only in which an appeal was not allowed, e.g. in sentences rendered *ex informata conscientia*, i.e., upon certified reliable information on the part of the responsible inferior, and in cases in which the Pope disallowed any appeal from the decision of the judge;[42]
3) a petition for restoration to a previous juridical status[43] and
4) any supplication presented to a sovereign when its expected accommodation was based not on strict claims of law, but on the benevolent equity and gra-

[38] N. (23. 1)

[39] C. (1. 19) 5.

[40] Cf. Reiffenstuel, Lib. II, tit. 28, n. 21; Benedictus XIV, const. *Ad militantis Ecclesiae*, 30 mart. 1742, n. 38—*Codicis Iuris Canonici Fontes cura Emi. Petri Card. Gasparri editi* (9 vols., Romae [postea Civitate Vaticana]: Typis Polyglottis Vaticanis, 1923-1939), (Vols. VII-IX ed. cura et studio Emi. Iustiniani Serédi), n. 326—hereinafter this collection will be cited as *Fontes*; S.C.C., *Lucionen.*, 8 apr. 1848, ad 2—*Fontes*, n. 4104.

[41] *Praelectiones in Textum Iuris Canonici de Iudiciis Ecclesiasticis in Scholis Pont. Sem. Rom. Habitae* (4 vols., Romae, 1896—1901), nn. 656, 657, 658—hereinafter cited *De Iudiciis Ecclesiasticis.*

[42] Lega pointed to this as the proper use of the term "*recursus.*"

[43] "Magis proprie"—Lega, *De Iudiciis Ecclesiasticis*, I, n. 657.

cious humanity of the one whom the petitioner besought.

There seemed to be a certain degree of difference between recourse and any kind of supplication. Supplication was an extraordinary remedy which was to be employed only when the use of all other means of redress had been exhausted. It was based entirely on the benignity of the Sovereign Pontiff. Recourse, however, seemed to be an ordinary remedy for definite cases in which the use of any other remedy was not available.[44] Moreover, recourse was in no sense an entreaty for kindness, but a strict plea for justice or at least for equity in the issue which was submitted to the sovereign's consideration.

B. *Present Remedy*

Instead of the twofold remedy provided by the previous law, the Code allows only one means of redress against the extrajudicial acts of superiors, the recourse.

The word *"recursus"* and its derivatives have no strict specialized meaning in the Code. In one canon[45] the word is used in the sense of a supplication,[46] such as may be made by a person who feels that he is being treated unfairly by a judge. In other places[47] recourse signifies the direction of a petition

[44] "... in veteri quoque disciplina, recursus seu expostulatio ad Apostolicam Sedem, ab appellatione extraiudiciali videbatur distingui, non qua mera supplicatio ad gratiam Principis impetrandam, sed qua remedium ordinarium, loco appellationis, ex iustitia vel saltem aequitate competens."—S.C.C., *Romana et aliarum,* 12 ian. 1924, *Animadversiones—Acta Apostolicae Sedis, Commentarium Officiale* (Romae, 1909—),XVI (1924), 164—hereinafter this organ will be cited as AAS; Noval, *Commentarium Codicis Iuris Canonici,* Lib. IV, *De Processibus* (2 vols., Romae: Marietti, 1920-1932), II, n. 509—hereinafter cited as *De Processibus.*

[45] Can. 1569, § 2: "Recursus tamen ad Sedem Apostolicam interpositus non suspendit, excluso casu appellationis, exercitium iurisdictionis in iudice qui causam iam cognoscere coepit . . .".

[46] Roberti, *De Processibus* (2 vols. in 1, Romae: apud Aedes Facultatis Iuridicae S. Apollinaris, 1926), II, n. 460; Beste, *Introductio in Codicem* (2 ed., Collegeville, Minn.: St. John's Abbey Press, 1944), p. 773—hereinafter cited as *Introductio.*

[47] Can. 2254, § 2: "Nihil impedit quominus poenitens . . . facto recursu ad Superiorem, alium adeat confessarium facultate praeditum . . ." See also cans. 2252 and 2290, §§ 1 & 2.

to a competent superior for his mandates concerning a censure which was absolved when the penitent was in danger of death, or in some very urgent case, by a priest who under ordinary circumstances would have lacked the power to grant the absolution. In still other canons[48] various forms of the verb *"recurrere"* are used in the meaning simply of an approach to a superior. Finally, the term "recourse" denotes a remedy or a means of redress against the extrajudicial acts of a superior.[49] Fundamentally every use of this word in the Code contemplates a subject's approach to some one constituted in authority.

In the present dissertation the term "recourse" is used in the meaning of a juridical remedy, or of a juridical means of redress. It may be defined as a plea made to a competent superior with a view to its possible unfavorable reflection upon the extrajudicial acts of a lesser superior, inasmuch as the one who presents the plea either claims or at least opines that he has suffered injury in his rights or detriment in his status.[50] The purpose of this remedy is to obtain the correction or the revocation of the acts of the lesser superior.

Recourse implies the exercise of a person's right to defend himself against probable or possible injustice or injury. Since this right of defense derives from the natural law itself, one may say that in substance the possibility of seeking recourse is a postulate of the natural law, while in its form, that is, in

[48] Cans. 48, § 3; 81; 429, § 5; 521, § 2; 583, 2°; 2334, 2°.

[49] Cans. 192, § 3; 296, § 2; 298; 345; 454, § 5; 498; 513, § 2; 647, § 2, 4°; 699, § 1; 880, § 2; 970; 1340, § 3; 1395, § 2; 1428, § 3; 1465, § 1; 1601; 1709, § 3; 1710; 1805; 2146, § 1; 2153, § 1; 2194; 2243, §§ 1 & 2; 2287.

[50] "Recursus dicitur provocatio a Superiore inferioris gradus ad Superiorem altioris gradus. Recursus datur ab actibus positis in ordine administrativo."—Roberti, *De Delictis et Poenis* Vol. I (ed. altera, Romae: Libraria Pontificii Instituti Utriusque Iuris, 1938), n. 288; ". . . quo apud superiorem altioris gradus contra suum ordinarium conqueritur in ordine ad obtinendam correctionem, emendationem vel etiam revocationem ordinationis sibi adversae. Talis provocatio vel expostulatio proprio nomine a Codice insignitur 'recursus,' si interponatur contra dispositiones administrativas seu provisiones extraiudiciales . . ."—Beste, *Introductio*, p. 773.

the formalities which must attend it, the possibility of seeking the recourse effectively is a benefit granted by human positive law.[51] Every man has the right to protect himself against probable and possible violation of any of his rights. It is positive human law that determines how he is to exercise this protection and defense. Hence every complete legal system, both ecclesiastical and civil, includes remedies to be used by members of society against the possible judicial and extrajudicial violations of their rights.

In Canon Law appeal is the ordinary means available against such possible violations through sentences pronounced by the judicial authorities in Church government.[52] Recourse is the extrajudicial counterpart of appeal. It is the remedy established by positive ecclesiastical law against the extrajudicial acts, decrees, ordinations, dispositions, decisions and transactions of superiors and against elections and the extrajudicial decisions of judges.

Recourse is not always concerned with a strict right. In many cases it is indeed concerned with the violations of strict rights, such as that of a pastor to retain his parish,[53] or that of a religious to remain in the community.[54] However, many recourses deal with the interest or the concern of the party, rather than with a strict right. The Code makes it clear that the local ordinary has no strict right to prevent the religious superior from removing a religious pastor from office; yet the ordinary can have a recourse in this matter.[55] Again, no priest has a strict right to be licensed to preach; yet when the Ordinary revokes this license, recourse may be made.[56] Consequently, one may say that recourse is concerned with both the rights and the interests of subjects.[57]

[51] Cf. Pirhing, Lib. II, tit. 28, n. 4; Lega, *De Iudiciis Ecclesiasticis*, I, n. 619.

[52] Can. 1879.

[53] Can. 2146.

[54] Can. 647, § 2.

[55] Can. 454, § 5.

[56] Can. 1340, § 3.

[57] Cf. Coronata, *Institutiones Iuris Canonici* (5 vols., Taurini: Marietti, 1928-1936), I, n. 333, 2°—hereinafter cited *Institutiones*.

Recourse is neither extrajudicial appeal nor supplication. The Code abolished the former institute of extrajudicial appeal as such, although it retained some of its characteristics in particular cases.[58]

Modern recourse lacks the formalities of extrajudicial appeal. Extrajudicial appeal was addressed to the metropolitan, patriarch or primate,[59] while recourse is usually made to the Holy See.[60] A ten day time limit was established for the lodging of an extrajudicial appeal,[61] but in the matter of recourse the law does not specify (except in a few particular cases) any limitation of time within which a recourse must be made if it is to receive a hearing. Consequently, those post-Code authors who identify recourse with extrajudicial appeal seem to be incorrect.[62]

On the other hand, recourse likewise is not identical with supplication. Recourse is based on justice and equity; it does not merely look to the benignity of the sovereign, as did supplication. A pastor who has been removed from office makes his recourse to the Holy See,[63] in order that he may be reinstated in his parish, and he seeks this reinstatement not as a favor from the Holy See, but as a matter of justice. Furthermore, recourse is the ordinary means of redress against the extrajudicial acts of superiors, whereas supplication was an extraordinary remedy in relation to both judicial and extrajudicial acts. Finally, the sphere of recourse is more limited than was that of supplication, which latter was concerned with any matter, even with petitions for favors and with pleas against the execution of judicial sentences.

[58] Cf. cans. 162, § 2; 1610, § 3; 1709, § 3.

[59] Cf. c. 3, C. II, q. 6—Jaffé, n. 109.

[60] Can. 1601.

[61] Cf. c. 28, C. II, q. 6; c. 8, *de appellationibus*, II, 15 in VI°.

[62] Prümmer, *Manuale Iuris Canonici* (3 ed., Friburgi Brisgoviae, 1922), q. 522—hereinafter cited *Manuale;* Roberti, *De Processibus*, I, n. 191; Vermeersch-Creusen, *Epitome Iuris Canonici* (3 vols., Mechliniae: H. Dessain, 1934-1937) (Vol. I, 6. ed., 1937; Vol. II, 5. ed., 1934; Vol. III, 6. ed., 1936), III, n. 237—hereinafter cited *Epitome;* Romani, *Summa Iuris Canonici Lineamenta* (Romae: Ex typographia Missionaria Dominicana, 1939), p. 213.

[63] Can. 2146, § 1.

However, recourse has characteristics in common both with supplication and with extrajudicial appeal. Like extrajudicial appeal, it is based on justice and equity, and both these canonical institutes deal or dealt with the same matters, viz. the extrajudicial acts of superiors and judges, elections, the care of souls, etc. In some cases, specified in law, there exists for the making of recourse the same limited period of time (*fatalia*)[64] as for the making of extrajudicial appeal. Like supplication, recourse is of an informal character, is usually addressed simply to the sovereign, and ordinarily can be invoked also outside of a fixed limited duration of time. Moreover, it generally is accompanied with a non-suspensive effect, which effect was common to both supplication and extrajudicial appeal.

It seems that recourse partakes more of the nature of supplication than of the nature of extrajudicial appeal.[65] It has more in common with supplication than with extrajudicial appeal, since in most instances it follows the pre-Code norms for the former rather than those for the latter. Moreover, as was previously noted in the present chapter, its origin is to be found in supplication.

Recourse differs in many points from judicial appeal. Recourse may be made from many kinds of actions, while appeal may be made from a definitive sentence only.[66] Appeal must be made within ten days of the notification of the publication of the sentence,[67] but a similar limited duration of time is generally not set as an imperative or essential condition for the making of a recourse. Appeal may be made orally[68] but

[64] Cans. 1465, § 1 and 2153; by declaration of the Roman Congregations, cans. 647, § 2, 4° and 2146, § 3.

[65] ". . . non videtur recursui, praesertim ad Sedem Apostolicam, aptandum simpliciter esse, quod de appellatione extraiudiciali (quae per Codicem videtur sublata) vetus ius statuebat. Enimvero recursus ad Apostolicam Sedem magis participat de supplicatione quam de appellatione."—S.C.C., *Romana et aliarum*, 12 ian. 1924, *Animadversiones*—AAS, XVI (1924), 164. Cf. Reiffenstuel, Lib. II, tit. 28, n. 21.

[66] Cans. 1879; 1880.

[67] Can. 1881.

[68] Can. 1882, § 1.

recourse must always be made in writing.[69] Appeal must always be made before the judge of the court from which the plea is carried to a higher tribunal (*iudex a quo*), [70] but there is no such requirement for initiating a recourse.

Usually, recourse does not suspend the decree, act, precept, disposition, etc.[71] against which it is made, while an appeal is usually *in suspensivo*.[72] In practically every case [73] recourse is made to the Holy See, but appeal is usually made from the tribunal of a suffragan to that of the metropolitan.[74] The matter which lends itself to the making of a judicial appeal becomes a judicially closed issue (*res iudiciata*) when two conformable sentences have been rendered;[75] the matter which underlies the use of a recourse never reaches a similar point of definitive and irrevocable settlement. Finally, there is the possibility of a second judicial appeal in the same matter to the Sacred Roman Rota,[76] while only one recourse may be made in any given case, unless new proofs have become available in support of the standing contention.

Recourse may originate from a judicial as well as from an extrajudicial background. The former of these two possibilities must be contemplated in necessary connection with the nonjudicial acts of an ecclesiastical judge. When he rejects a plaintiff's bill of complaint (*libellus*), the party concerned may not make an appeal, for an appeal is referrible to a sentence, and no sentence has been rendered in this case. In rejecting the bill of complaint the judge acts in an administrative way, and consequently the remedy to be invoked against him is that of recourse.[77]

In like manner the remedy against a judge's declaration

[69] Cf. *infra*, p. 37.

[70] Can. 1881.

[71] Cf. *infra*. pp. 102-118.

[72] Can. 1889, § 2.

[73] The exceptions are listed in cans. 162, § 2; 1610, § 3; 1709, § 3; 1710; 2153, § 1.

[74] Can. 1594, § 1.

[75] Can. 1902, 1°.

[76] Can. 1559, § 1, 2°, and § 2.

[77] Can. 1709, § 3.

that he is relatively incompetent to hear a case,[78] and against a judge's failure to accept or reject a bill of complaint,[79] is a recourse. In these three instances and also in other recourses from the nonjudicial acts of judges there is established the possible making of a recourse that differs from the usual extrajudicial recourse. In the cases of recourse which originate from a judicial background the superior *ad quem* is not the administrative superior of the ordinary, i.e., the Holy See, but the usual court of judicial appeal, i.e., the superior tribunal. The present dissertation will consider these "judicial" recourses in an incidental way only. Similarly, it will deal in a merely indirect way with the recourse which may be invoked by an elector when he was not called for his rightful participation in an election.[80] The particular and primary interest of this paper centers in recourses from the actions of ordinaries and superiors, not from the actions of judges or of persons who in law are held responsible for notifying all qualified electors regarding the set time of a prospective election.

[78] Can. 1610, § 3.
[79] Can. 1710.
[80] Can. 162, § 2.

CHAPTER II

MATTER OF THE RECOURSE

A. *Non-judicial Powers of the Superior a Quo*

Since recourse is a legal remedy against the extrajudicial acts of superiors, it is necessary to have a knowledge of the powers of superiors if one is to have a complete knowledge of the remedy.

As soon as he has canonically taken possession of his office, a residential Bishop has the right to govern his diocese in both spiritual and temporal matters with legislative, judicial and coactive powers.[1] Episcopal powers are considered by the Code under the headings of judicial and non-judicial jurisdiction.[2] Non-judicial power, which is also called voluntary jurisdiction[3] includes legislative, administrative and coactive powers.[4]

[1] Can. 335, § 1.

[2] Can. 201, §§ 2-3.

[3] "Nisi aliud ex rerum natura aut ex iure constet, potestatem voluntariam seu non-iudicialem . . ."—Can. 201, § 3.

[4] Some authors feel that voluntary power is that which is exercised in favor of someone who seeks or wishes that power—thus, e.g., Chelodi, *Ius de Personis iuxta Codicem Iuris Canonici* (ed. altera. a Sac. Ernesto Bertagnolli recognita et aucta, Tridenti: Libr. Edit. Tridentum, 1927), n. 125; Oesterle, *Praelectiones Iuris Canonici*, I, (Romae: Ex Officina Typographica "Cuore di Maria," 1931), 110. They regard voluntary jurisdiction as opposed to contentious. Their viewpoint was admissible in pre-Code law but the law of the Code in using the phrase "*voluntariam seu non-iudicialem*" seems to make voluntary jurisdiction synonymous with non-judicial; hence most authors say that jurisdiction is called voluntary because it lacks the formalities of judicial procedure in which the adverse claims of contending parties are submitted for authoritative settlement; in other words, it abstracts from the need of following any specified form of procedure. These latter authors say also that voluntary jurisdiction embraces legislative, administrative and coactive powers.—Thus, e.g., Wernz-Vidal, *Ius Canonicum* (7 vols. in 8, Romae: Universitas Gregoriana, 1923-1938), I, n. 375, b; Coronata, *Institutiones*, I, n. 282, c; Toso, *Ad Codicem Iuris Canonici Commentaria Minora*, Vol. 1 (Taurini, Marietti, 1921), pp. 172 and 174—hereinafter cited as *Commentaria Minora;* Cocchi, *Commentarium in Codicem Iuris Canonici ad Usum Scholarum* (8 vols., Taurini: Marietta, 1920-1930), II, n. 116—herein-

Since the present dissertation is not concerned in any direct way with the judicial power of ordinaries, there is no need for any particular consideration of that power. The following considerations are accordingly concerned with the non-judicial powers of superiors.

By his legislative power is meant the ordinary's right to propose in an obligatory manner whatever he deems necessary for the attainment of the purpose of the Church in his diocese.[5] The object of this power is to reform morals, to restore discipline, to promote divine worship, to order public and private prayers, and, in general, to procure the good government of the diocese.[6] The ordinary may make laws either in the diocesan synod,[7] or at any other time. The laws that he promulgates are usually called statutes, decrees, or constitutions.[8] The matter of his laws must always be either in direct harmony with (*secundum ius*) or in non-oppositional addition

after cited as *Commentarium;* Woywod, *A Practical Commentary on the Code of Canon Law* (5. ed. revised, 2 vols., New York: Joseph F. Wagner, 1939), I, n. 155—hereinafter cited as *Commentary;* Sipos, *Enchiridion Iuris Canonici* (2. ed., Pécs: "Haladás R. T.", 1931), p. 155—hereinafter cited as *Enchiridion.* For a discussion of the differences between judicial and voluntary jurisdictions, see Meier, *Penal Administrative Procedure Against Negligent Pastors,* The Catholic University of America Canon Law Studies, n. 140, (Washington, D. C., The Catholic University of America Press, 1941) pp. 86-89.

[5] Cappello, *Summa Iuris Publici Ecclesiastici ad Normam Codicis Iuris Canonici et Recentiorum S. Sedis Documentorum Concinnata* (2. ed., Romae: apud Aedes Universitatis Gregorianae, 1928), n. 61—hereinafter cited as *Summa Iuris Publici;* Ottaviani, *Institutiones Iuris Publici Ecclesiastici* (2. ed., 2 vols., Civitate Vaticana: Typis Polyglottis Vaticanis, 1935-1936), I, n. 42—hereinafter cited as *Institutiones;* Ryan, *Principles of Episcopal Jurisdiction,* The Catholic University of America Canon Law Studies, n. 120 (Washington, D. C.: The Catholic University of America Press, 1939), p. 121.

[6] De Meester, *Juris Canonici et Juris Canonico-Civilis Compendium* (ed. nova, 3 vols. in 4, Brugis, 1921-1928), II, n. 678—hereinafter cited as *Compendium.*

[7] Can. 362.

[8] Cf. cans. 22; 360, § 2; 362: Coronata, *Institutiones,* I, n. 414, 3°.

to (*praeter ius*) the existing common law. It may not run counter to (*contra*) that law.[9]

Connected with his legislative power is the ordinary's right to impose precepts.[10] A precept is defined as a reasonable command given to individuals by a competent superior.[11] It is not a mere exhortation, but a command inducing a moral obligation. The matter of the precept must be just, possible of performance and either useful or necessary. In its duration a precept may be either perpetual or temporary.[12] Usually, however, it ceases with the fulfillment of the task assigned, or with the loss of power on the part of the one who gave it, unless it was imposed through a legitimate document or in the presence of two witnesses.[13]

Precepts may be given not only to an individual, but even to a group of individuals. Michiels[14] regards precepts given to a group in two ways: either as given to the members as individuals, or as given to the community as a group. When the precept is given to the members as individuals, it is equivalent to a singular precept given to each member. When it is given to the members as a group, then, if the group is one which is capable of receiving a law, if the superior giving the precept has legislative power and if there is attached to the precept a definite degree of stability, the precept is for all practical purposes the equivalent of a law.

Coactive power may be defined as the right to use force in order to compel compliance from those who are reluctant in their obedience to laws and precepts, to restrain the transgressors of laws, and to punish the contumacious and delinquent members of society, so that these persons will not be free to transgress laws and disregard decrees without penal

[9] ". . . ad normam sacrorum canonum exercenda."—Can. 335, § 1. Cf. Coronata, *Institutiones*, I, n. 394, 1°.

[10] Wernz-Vidal, *Ius Canonicum*, II, n. 599, 1, a.

[11] ". . . iussum rationabile a competente Superiore singulis datum." —Michiels, *Normae Generales Iuris Canonici* (2 vols., Lublin: Universitas Catholica, 1929), I, 507—hereinafter cited as *Normae Generales*.

[12] Coronata, *Institutiones*, I, n. 31; Sipos, *Enchiridion*, p. 24.

[13] Can. 24.

[14] *Normae Generales*, I, 519.

consequences.[15] In the Church coactive power is exemplified through the infliction of either spiritual or temporal penalties.[16] The transfer of an episcopal or parochial see from one location to another by way of penalty, the deprival of or the suspension of a cleric from receiving an ecclesiastical pension, and the imposition of pecuniary fines[17] are examples of temporal penalties in Church Law. Excommunication, interdict and suspension[18] are spiritual penalties.

His coactive power gives an ordinary the right to use these spiritual and temporal penalties in order to constrain his subjects to the fulfillment of the aim for which ecclesiastical society exists.[19] He has the right to apply the penalties stipulated by the common law, and even to establish penalties which will be incurred either as *latae* or *ferendae sententiae* penalties for the violation of certain specified laws or precepts.[20] He may, moreover, establish a penalty, or intensify a penalty already established, for the violation not only of his own or his predecessors' laws, but even of the laws of his superiors or of God Himself.[21]

Furthermore, the ordinary, as the guardian of ecclesiastical discipline in his territory, has the right and the duty to watch over the application of the universal and particular laws which bind his subjects in common.[22] This is generally called

[15] Cf. Esswein, *The Extrajudicial Coercive Powers of Ecclesiastical Superiors*, The Catholic University of America Canon Law Studies, n. 127 (Washington, D. C.: The Catholic University of America Press, 1941), p. 3; Cappello, *Summa Iuris Publici*, n. 68; Ryan, *Principles of Episcopal Jurisdiction*, p. 124.

[16] "Nativum et proprium Ecclesiae ius est, independens a qualibet humana auctoritate, coercendi delinquentes sibi subditos poenis tum spiritualibus tum temporalibus."—Can. 2214, § 1.

[17] Can. 2291, 3°, 7°, 12°.

[18] Can. 2255, § 1.

[19] Cavagnis, *Institutiones Iuris Publici Ecclesiastici Quas in Scholis Pontificii Seminarii Romani tradidit* (2 vols. in 1, Romae, 1882), I, n. 140—hereinafter cited as *Institutiones;* Coronata, *Ius Publicum Ecclesiasticum* (2. ed., Taurini: Marietti, 1934), n. 22, c.

[20] Can. 2220, § 1.

[21] Can. 2221.

[22] "Observantiam legum ecclesiasticarum Episcopi urgent . . ."—Can. 336, § 1.

his executive power. The specific purpose of this power is the "authoritative direction of persons and the authoritative administration of material means or temporalities, both of which may be effected when necessary by the use of physical force, spiritual or temporal coercion."[23] The aim of executive power in the hands of the ordinary is the immediate and practical application of all laws that are in force in the diocese. This power may be used either in close conjunction with (*secundum legem*) or in kindred supplementation to (*praeter legem*) the existing law. In the former of these possibilities the ordinary applies and enforces the laws as instituted by higher legislators for a universal diocesan application; in the latter he applies and enforces the diocesan laws which he and his predecessors have promulgated.[24]

Authors consider that coercive or coactive power is actually a subdivision of this executive power.[25] The other subdivision they call administrative power.[26] With this latter power the ordinary superintends the temporalities which pertain to the episcopal office, and watches over the management and control of parochial and other ecclesiastical goods in his territory.[27] By means of it he erects,[28] unites,[29] divides,[30] and confers[31] benefices; he incardinates clerics into his diocese;[32] watches over the control of ecclesiastical temporal goods and prescribes the norms for their management and use;[33] exacts tributes;[34] sets funeral fees[35] and determines the amount

[23] Ryan, *Principles of Episcopal Jurisdiction*, p. 143.

[24] Cf. Ryan, *loc. cit.*

[25] Cavagnis, *Institutiones*, I, n. 99; *Cappello, Summa Iuris Publici*, nn. 60 and 64; Coronata, *Ius Publicum Ecclesiasticum*, n. 22, c.

[26] Cavagnis, *loc. cit.*; Cappello, *loc. cit.*; Sipos, *Enchiridion*, p. 239.

[27] "Loci Ordinarii est sedulo advigilare administrationi omnium bonorum ecclesiasticorum quae in suo territorio sint nec ex eius iurisdictione fuerint subducta . . ."—Can. 1519, § 1.

[28] Can. 1414, § 2.

[29] Can. 1423, § 1.

[30] Can. 1427, § 1.

[31] Cans. 152; 403; 1432, § 1.

[32] Cans. 112; 114; 117.

[33] Cans. 1478; 1519, §§ 1-2.

[34] Cans. 1056; 1355; 1504; 1505; 1506.

[35] Can. 1234, § 1.

of the offering receivable as a Mass stipend.[36] The ordinary's decisions in matters subject to his executive and administrative powers are usually formulated as decrees.[37]

Canonists, however, do not always refer to this branch of executive power when they speak of administrative power. "To administer" means literally to apply something to another. Hence Noval (1861-1938) stated:

> "Hoc sensu quaelibet ex tribus speciebus publicae potestatis, scilicet, tam potestas legislativa quam iudicialis et executiva, dicitur administrare, et quilibet actus earum dicitur administrativus, et quaevis actuum series ab iisdem peracta sub certis solemnitatibus diceretur processus administrativus; nam potestas legislativa ministrat sodalibus normas agendi, potestas iudicialis declarationem practicam iurium, potestas executiva executionem legum, sententiarum et decretorum, in summa, quarumcumque normarum agendi socialium."[38]

A proper example of this wide meaning of the term "administrative power" is to be found in the wording of Canon 431, § 2, where the one who in particular circumstances is called on to assume charge of a vacant diocese is designated as its administrator. Actually this cleric has the full episcopal jurisdiction of an ordinary except in certain cases specified by law.[39] The Code elsewhere supports this use of the term

[36] Can. 831, § 1.

[37] "Decretum . . . diverso sensu adhibetur. Hoc nomine designantur decisiones SS. Congregationum, pronuntiationes iudicum . . . acta gubernationis Episcoporum et aliorum qui auctoritate publica gaudent in Ecclesia. Hoc ultimo sensu intellecta, decreta sunt decisiones latae in casu particulari, vi potestatis, non legislativae vel iudiciariae, sed gubernativae et executivae, et possunt vocari praecepta data communitati vel singulis, quibus vel lex exsecutioni mandatur, vel quid novi et specialis iniungitur."—Van Hove, *Commentarium Lovaniense in Codicem Iuris Canonici*, Vol. II, *De Legibus Ecclesiasticis* (Mechliniae, H. Dessain, 1930), n. 371, 2°.

[38] *De Processibus*, II, n. 461.

[39] Can. 435, § 1. Cf. Jaeger, *The Administration of Vacant and Quasi-Vacant Episcopal Sees in the United States*, The Catholic Uni-

"administrative power", since it speaks of administrators apostolic,[40] who, if permanently constituted, have the same rights and obligations as a residential bishop.[41]

In order to achieve a full clarity of expression, and thus ensure a correct understanding of his meaning, the writer proposes henceforth to use the term "administrative power" in the sense of legislative, executive and coactive powers. To designate the subdivision of executive power which some authors call "administrative power," he will use the phrase "executive administrative power," or some other equivalently specific phrase.

It is constantly to be borne in mind that all the powers of the ordinary are to be used in accordance with the norms set by law (*ad normam iuris*),[42] since his is not a supreme jurisdiction but rather a subordinate one which is subject to limits and not fully independent of all higher authority in the Church.[43] If an ordinary should formulate a statute, a decree or a sentence, or if he should impose a precept or a penalty which is contrary to the common law, or which does not correspond to the requirements of the common law, his action would be invalid and devoid of legal consequences.

In clerical exempt religious institutes the major superiors along with the chapters of these institutes have ordinary jurisdictional powers over their subjects.[44] In general, this jurisdiction embraces the legislative, judicial and executive powers which belong to episcopal authority, except in such matters which are incompatible with the religious state (e.g., jurisdiction to adjudicate matrimonial cases) or are reserved to the

versity of America Canon Law Studies, n. 81 (Washington, D. C.: The Catholic University of America, 1932), pp. 167-175.

[40] Cans. 312-315.

[41] Can. 315.

[42] Can. 335, § 1.

[43] "Romani Rontificis potestas summa est, universalis, planeque sui iuris, episcoporum vero certis circumscripta finibus, nec plane sui iuris." —Leo XIII, ep. encycl., *Satis cognitum*, 29 iunii 1896, n. 31—*Fontes*, n. 630.

[44] "Superiores et Capitula . . . in religione autem clericali exempta, habent iurisdictionem ecclesiasticam tam pro foro interno, quam pro externo."—Can. 501, § 1.

Holy See or to the local ordinary.[45] However, this jurisdiction must always be exercised according to the constitutions of the community.[46] Religious ordinaries may not make statutes or decrees or give precepts which are not in accord, at least implicitly and indirectly, with the constitutions of the institute itself.[47] Their decrees, statutes and precepts must not run counter to, intensify or weaken the purport of the rule to which the community is subject,[48] by ordering, for example, that one of their subjects accept an appointment to the foreign missions. Such an ordinance given to a subject of a non-missionary community would plainly be beyond the constitutions of the community.

In all communities, whether exempt or non-exempt, clerical or lay, the superiors together with the chapters or councils have a dominative power.[49] Clancy[50] defines dominative power in religious institutes as "that authority which a superior has over his subjects in virtue of their enrollment in the community, and by reason of which he governs their actions, within limits defined by the Code of Canon Law and the particular Constitutions of the institute, to the attainment of the end or purpose of the society." It is, then, a private power in sharp contrast to jurisdiction, which is a public power in the sense that it is exercised by one having public authority.[51]

[45] Fanfani, *De Iure Religiosorum ad Normam Codicis Iuris Canonici* (ed. altera, Taurini: Marietti, 1925), n. 51, B—hereinafter cited as *De Iure Religiosorum;* Papi, *The Government of Religious Communities* (New York, 1919), n. 55; Pejška, *Ius Canonicum Religiosorum* (3. ed., Friburgi Brisgoviae: Herder, 1927), p. 139.

[46] "Supremus religionis Moderator potestatem obtinet in omnes provincias, domos, sodales religionis, *exercendam secundum constitutiones;* alii Superiores ea gaudent infra fines sui muneris."—Can. 502 (Italics inserted). Cf. cans. 501, § 1; 532, § 1.

[47] Fanfani, *De Iure Religiosorum,* n. 51, B.

[48] Pejška, *Ius Canonicum Religiosorum,* p. 141: ". . . contra vel supra vel infra regulam."

[49] "Superiores et Capitula, ad normam constitutionum et iuris communis, potestatem habent dominativam in subditos . . ."—Can. 501, § 1.

[50] *The Local Religious Superior,* The Catholic University of America Canon Law Studies, n. 175 (Washington, D. C.: The Catholic University of America Press, 1943), p. 8.

Those who have only dominative power lack true legislative, judicial and executive authority, since these powers are associable only with the power of jurisdiction. Superiors who act simply in virtue of dominative power must use paternal methods. They may impose precepts[52] which entail a moral obligation. The "statutes" of such superiors or chapters, when given to the entire religious institute, are not true laws, but rather partake of the nature of precepts given to a community.[53] Since they lack jurisdiction, superiors with only dominative power may not inflict canonical penalties, nor may they attach canonical penalties to the violation of their statutes or precepts. They do, however, have the right to impose penal remedies and penances.[54]

B. *Recourse in Relation to These Powers of Superiors*

a. *Pre-Code Discipline*

Under the pre-Code discipline a supplication could be invoked against any allegedly inequitable action of a superior or even of an equal in the Church. It was immaterial whether the action of the superior which gave rise to the supplication was of a legislative, judicial or executive character.[54] One

[51] Some authors distinguish between dominative and domestic (or social) power. The former, they say, derives radically from the free submission of the will of the person who enters a religious institute; the latter, through the natural law, belongs to the head of any subordinate society.—Cf. Schaefer, *De Religiosis ad normam Codicis Iuris Canonici* (3. ed., Romae: S.A.L.E.R., 1940), n. 108, 1—hereinafter cited as *De Religiosis;* Bakalarczyk, *De Novitiatu,* The Catholic University of America Canon Law Studies, n. 36 (Washington, D. C.: The Catholic University of America, 1927), p. 146. But, as Pejška says (*Ius Canonicum Religiosorum,* p. 119), this distinction will at times prove cumbersome. To insist on this distinction would serve no practical purpose in this present study.

[52] Coronata, *Institutiones,* I, n. 32, 1°; Vermeersch-Creusen, *Epitome,* I, n. 105; Van Hove, *De Legibus Ecclesiasticis,* n. 353; Michiels, *Normae Generales,* I, 507; Sipos, *Enchiridion,* p. 24.

[53] Cf. Schaefer, *De Religiosis,* n. 107, f; Michiels, *Normae Generales,* I, 519.

[54] Schaefer, *De Religiosis,* n. 107, f; Coronata, *Institutiones,* I, n. 32, 1°.

[55] Reiffenstuel, Lib. II, tit. 28, n. 18; Schmalzgrueber, Lib. II, tit. 28, n. 5.

could present a supplication even in matters in which an extrajudicial appeal was forbidden, e.g., in a suspension which had been inflicted in view of an ordinary's private and personal knowledge (*ex informata conscientia*).[56]

Extrajudicial appeal, however, was available only within a more limited scope, since it was not a means of seeking redress against a superior's judicial acts. It bore a possible relation to any and all extrajudicial acts of ordinaries and superiors. The list of matters in which one could appeal extrajudicially was quite large, since it potentially included every kind of injury suffered outside court procedure. It was the available remedy not only against injuries already suffered, but also against injuries that were feared as impending.[57] Extrajudicial appeals could be employed with reference to elections and postulations,[58] to matters connected with benefices,[59] to episcopal decrees,[60] to corrections and censures,[61] to decrees given at the time of visitation as well as to the visitation itself,[62] and to any other extrajudicial matter.

b. *Present Discipline*

When post-Code authors speak of administrative recourse, they do not mean to limit the application of this remedy to the acts of the executive administrative power. They use the word "administrative" in a wider sense to include the nonjudicial powers of the ordinary.[63] This is evident when one

[56] Benedictus XIV, const. *Ad militantis Ecclesiae*, 30 mart. 1742, n. 23 —*Fontes*, n. 326; S.C.C., *Lucionen.*, 8 apr. 1848, ad 2—*Fontes*, n. 4104.

[57] C. 51, X, *de appellationibus, recusationibus, et relationibus*, II, 28.

[58] C. 4, *de electione et electi potestate*, I, 6, in VI°; c. 3, *de electione et electi potestate*, I, 3, in Clem.

[59] Benedictus XIV, const. *Ad militantis Ecclesiae*, 30 mart. 1742, nn. 9, 12, 16, 22, etc.—*Fontes*, n. 326.

[60] *Ad militantis Ecclesiae*, nn. 6, 7, 8, etc.; Leo XIII, const. *Romanos Pontifices*, 8 maii 1881—*Fontes*, n. 582; S.C.C., *Hydruntina*, 14 iunii 1594 —*Fontes*, n. 2269.

[61] *Ad militantis Ecclesiae*, nn. 12, 14; S.C.Ep. et Reg., decr. 16 oct. 1600, n. 8—*Fontes*, n. 1586.

[62] *Ad militantis Ecclesiae*, nn. 10, 21; S.C.C., *Barbastren.*, 28 nov. 1602—*Fontes*, n. 2347; S.C.C., *Segobricen.*, 24 aug. 1605—*Fontes*, n. 2358.

[63] Noval, *De Processibus*, II, n. 461.

considers the variety of matters in which the Code expressly states that non-judicial recourse may be invoked.

Recourse is certainly applicable in cases wherein the executive power of the ordinary has been used. The Code expressly mentions recourse as the available means of redress against the ordinary's act of depriving a removable[64] or an irremovable incumbent of his office;[65] against the mandates of a vicar or prefect apostolic regarding the care of souls, the administration of the sacraments, the direction of schools, the disposal of offerings made in behalf of some particular mission, and the fulfillment of last wills or testaments made in pious favor of such a mission;[66] against the decrees of a vicar or prefect apostolic as issued by him in settlement of controversies existing between individual missionaries, between religious societies or also between the missionaries and outside persons in reference to the care of souls;[67] against the decrees of authorized agents in conducting a canonical visitation;[68] against the dismissal of a religious in temporary vows;[69] against the local ordinary's suppression of an association of the faithful, whether it was erected by the ordinary's direct authority, or by the authority of religious in virtue of an indult from the Holy See, as long as the effective use of this indult postulated the ordinary's consent;[70] against the ordinary's proscription to a pastor or to a canon penitentiary regarding the function of hearing confessions;[71] against an ordinary's or a religious supe-

[64] Can. 192, § 3.

[65] Can. 2146, § 1.

[66] Can. 296, § 2.

[67] Can. 298.

[68] Cans. 345; 513, § 2.

[69] Can. 647, § 2, 4°. It is possible for such a dismissal to be effected either by means of the executive power (e.g., when the religious has not committed any delict, but has shown that he lacks the proper qualifications for community life) or by means of the coactive power.

[70] Can. 699, § 1. This suppression, likewise, may be decreed through the use either of the executive or of the coactive power.

[71] Can. 880, § 2. This act of proscription need not always be occasioned by a delict; it may follow in consequence of the deafness, scrupulosity, etc. of the one to whom the exercise of the function is denied.

rior's act of disallowing a cleric to ascend to higher orders;[72] against the ordinary's act of uniting, transferring, dividing or dismembering benefices;[73] against the rejection of a patron's second presentee for incumbency in a benefice,[74] and against other similar decrees which an ordinary may publish in the regulation of matters subject to his executive administrative power.[75] All the aforementioned matters relate in some way or other to the executive administrative power which the law entrusts to ordinaries for their proper supervision and management.

Recourse may also be had in cases that involve the use of legislative power. In pre-Code law the Constitution *Romanos Pontifices* of Leo XIII (1878-1903) dealt with the possibility of invoking recourse against the synodal decrees of bishops.[76] The Code itself speaks of recourse made against precepts;[77] we have already noted[78] that the imposition of precept is connected with the legislative power when the one who imposes the precept has jurisdiction. The Code speaks also of recourse made against the directive regulations enacted by vicars and prefects apostolic;[79] these regulations proceed from the legislative power.

Recourse may finally be employed against the exercise of the coactive power. This is evident from the fact that the Code speaks of recourse against censures[80] and vindicative penalties;[81] against the penal dismissal of religious in temporary vows;[82] against the penal proscription of the exercise of

[72] Can. 970. The denial of the cleric's desire to receive higher orders will usually imply the use of the coactive power, but there may be occasions when the ordinary's act of proscription points simply to the use of his executive power.

[73] Can. 1428, § 3.

[74] Can. 1465, § 1.

[75] Can. 1601.

[76] 8 maii 1881—*Fontes*, n. 582.

[77] Can. 2243, § 2.

[78] Cf. *supra* p. 19.

[79] Can. 296, § 2.

[80] Can. 2243, § 1.

[81] Can. 2287.

[82] Can. 647, § 2, 4°.

his confessional powers on the part of a pastor or of the canon penitentiary;[83] against the interdiction which bars a cleric from ascent to higher orders;[84] and against an ordinary's infliction of suspension under circumstances in which he acts upon private but definitely reliable knowledge (*ex informata conscientia*).[85]

It is clear that the legislator did not intend to limit the use of recourse as a legal remedy solely for these cases in connection with which the available use of this remedy is expressly mentioned. Rather, recourse is a general remedy which may be employed against any extrajudicial act of an ordinary.[86] Undeniable evidence of this is found in the fact that the Code does not qualify the words "*Ordinariorum decreta*" as incorporated in canon 1601. It has previously been shown[87] that decrees may originate from either the legislative or the executive power of an ordinary. Consequently it can be stated that recourse stands available as a remedy for possible use against any decree of an ordinary.

The cases for which the Code expressly mentions the availability of recourse are to be recognized, in a sense, as examples of the more generous use of recourse which the Code allows. The remedy may be used, for instance, not only against the ordinary's rejection of the patron's second presentee, but likewise against the ordinary's rejection of the patron's first presentee since it is the policy of the Holy See that the services of her Congregations are available to any of the faithful who invoke their aid.[88] For the same reason the use of recourse is not exclusively reserved to a religious in temporary vows when

[83] Can. 880, § 2.

[84] Can. 970.

[85] Can. 2194.

[86] Vermeersch-Creusen, *Epitome*, III, n. 237; Noval, *De Processibus*, I, n. 635; Beste, *Introductio*, p. 267; Suarez, *De Remotione Parochorum Aliisque Processibus Tertiae Partis Lib. IV C. I. C.* (Romae; Pontificium Internationale Institutum Angelicum de Urbe, 1931), n. 21—hereinafter cited as *De Remotione Parochorum*.

[87] Cf. *supra*, p. 18 and p. 22.

[88] Cf. *Ordo Servandus in Romana Curia—Normae Communes*, 29 iun. 1908, Cap. X, sect. 1, 1°—hereinafter cited as *Normae Communes*. Pistocchi, *De Re Beneficiali iuxta Canones* (Taurini: Marietti, 1928), p. 358.

he feels that an injustice has been done to him through his dismissal from a religious community; a similar use of recourse is available for a religious in perpetual vows when he feels that he has suffered a like grievance.[89]

May one make a recourse to the Holy See against the extrajudicial actions of a person who functions with vicarious ordinary power?[90] In other words, must the actions of a vicar general stand confirmed by the episcopal ordinary if recourse to Rome is to be possible in the case? In strict law there is no impediment to bar the use of recourse in such a case. But, so it seems to this writer, the more expeditious and practical method of reaching a solution suggests that the matter be presented to the ordinary for review. Such a step, it is true, does not strictly constitute the making of a recourse; rather, it implies simply the presentation of a plea for a rehearing of the facts in the case by the same juridical authority in the person of the bishop. If the latter countermands the action of his vicar general, then the plea has achieved its desired success; if he confirms the previous act, then the way for recourse to the Holy See is still open.

Recourse is available against the actions of superiors not only when they have exercised jurisdictional power, but also when they have functioned with merely dominative power. This is implied in the statement of the Code[91] that the Sacred Congregation of Religious is competent to deal with all questions of government or discipline in all religious communities or societies. This statement, unrestricted as it is, fully warrants the conclusion that this Congregation's competence extends also to matters of recourse which may be made by a

[89] Schaefer, *De Religiosis*, nn. 582, 583; Vermeersch, "Annotationes" —*Periodica de Religiosis et Missionariis*, 1905-1919; *Periodica de Re Canonica et Morali utili praesertim Religiosis et Missionariis*, 1920-1927; *Periodica de Re Canonica, Morali, Liturgica*, 1927—(Brugis), XII (1923-1924), 102—hereinafter cited as *Periodica;* O'Leary, *Religious Dismissed after Perpetual Profession*, The Catholic University of America Canon Law Studies, n. 184 (Washington, D. C.: The Catholic University of America Press, 1943) pp. 49, 50.

[90] Cf. can. 197, § 2.

[91] Can. 251, § 1.

member of a religious community or society in which the superiors actually exercise simply a dominative power. The availability of recourse against the use of dominative power is implied also when the Code[92] states that a religious in temporary vows may have a recourse against a decree of dismissal; in no way does the Code limit this right to recourse against the decree of dismissal, and consequently this recourse is available to religious in communities in which superiors have a dominative power only as well as to religious in communities in which superiors have a jurisdictional power. We conclude, therefore, that recourse may be employed against the injustices and injuries which result from the use of dominative power.

It must be borne in mind that there is no possibility of recourse against the decrees, precepts, acts, etc. of the Roman Pontiff. He is the sovereign of the Church. Over him there is no earthly superior, to whom the recourse could be made. No man has the right to sit in judgment on him or on his actions.[93] This principle is expressly exemplified in the statement of the Code which rules out the possibility of an appeal from a judicial sentence of the Pope.[94] There is no similar explicit statement in regard to the question of recourse. However, the impossibility of a recourse from a papal act is implied in the Code when it establishes an automatic penalty for anyone who seeks redress against the laws, decrees and mandates of the Roman Pontiff by submitting his plea to an ecumenical council.[95]

Against the decrees and mandates of the Sacred Congregations a twofold means of redress may be employed. There may be submitted to the Congregation itself a request for a new hearing,[96] or there may be a recourse to the Holy Father personally.[97]

[92] Can. 647, § 2, 4°.

[93] Can. 1556.

[94] Can. 1880, 1°.

[95] Can. 2332.

[96] Cf. in relation to judicial appeal, Coronata, *Institutiones*, III, n. 1409; Wernz-Vidal, *Ius Canonicum*, VI, nn. 604, 606; Beste, *Introductio*, p. 242.

[97] Cf. cans. 218, §§ 1-2, 1569, § 1.

CHAPTER III

MANNER OF MAKING A RECOURSE

A. *Pre-Code Discipline*

In pre-Code law the manner of making and prosecuting an extrajudicial appeal was similar to the procedure for judicial appeals. The appeal was made by notifying the superior or judge who had caused the injury (*iudex a quo*). In the case of a judicial appeal this notification could be made orally at the time of the pronouncement of the sentence,[1] but in the case of an extrajudicial appeal the notification had always to be made by means of a written claim.[2] The one who appealed had the option to do so personally or through a proxy.[3] The judge or the superior from whom the appeal was made then issued dimissorial letters (*apostoli*) which the appellant had to bring to the one to whom he appealed.[4] The *apostoli* issued for extrajudicial appeals were called *extraiudiciales* or *conventionales* or *testimoniales*.[5]

Gregory X (1271-1276) established a new procedure in regard to certain extrajudicial appeals.[6] He ordered that those who appealed against an election, postulation or assignment to office had to express in their written instrument of appeal everything that they intended to allege against the person or the form in the election, postulation or assignment. The appellants, moreover, were to swear that they knew that their objections were true, and that they could prove them. The fulfillment of these requirements was necessary for the validity of the appeal. If these demands were not complied with,

[1] *Dictum Gratiani* post c. 41, C. II, q. 6.

[2] *Glossa Ordinaria* s. v. *Quomodo sit appellandum*, c. 1, C. II, q. 6; c. 1, *de appellationibus*, II, 15, in VI°.

[3] C. 28, C. II, q. 6; N. (23. 1).

[4] Cc. 24, 31, C. II, q. 6; D. (49. 6) 1; c. 1, *de appellationibus*, II, 15, in VI°.

[5] Ioannes Andreae, as quoted in the *Additio* among the glosses on c. 1, *de appellationibus*, II, 15, in VI°; Panormitanus, tit. *de appellationibus*, (II, 51, 9).

[6] C. 4, *de electione et electi potestate*, I, 6, in VI°.

the appeal was not to be heard. Finally, the appellate judge (*iudex ad quem*) was to consider only those matters which were expressed in the sworn statement.

Boniface VIII (1294-1303) determined more specifically the oath which had been required by Gregory X. Boniface insisted[7] that it was not sufficient for the appellant to swear that he believed to be true either all the matters proposed in his written plea, or at least enough of them for repelling the claim of the elected, postulated or assigned incumbent in office. Such an oath was too disjunctive and appeared at the same time to be evasive. Boniface declared that the Gregorian statute demanded an oath, taken on the Gospels, that everything (with no exceptions or disjunctions) set forth in the instrument of appeal was true and could be established as such by means of proof. In another decretal[8] Boniface explained that the Gregorian statute applied to extrajudicial appeals only, and not to judicial appeals in matters of elections, postulations or assignments to office.

One who appealed in writing was not obliged to read his appeal to the superior or judge who had inflicted the injury (*iudex a quo*), since it sufficed that the formulation of the appeal be contained in the written plea (*libellus*).[9] Moreover, the superior or judge from whom the appeal was made could not compel the appellant to prove the existence of the injury which he allegedly suffered.[10]

At the Ecumenical Council of Vienne in 1312 Clement V (1305-1314) ordered that extrajudicial appeals, like their judicial counterparts, had to be prosecuted within one year from the day on which either the appeal was made or the injury was suffered (e.g., when the appeal was made from an injury that had not yet been suffered). If no just impediment prevented the prosecution of the appeal, it was to be regarded as deserted when it had not been completed within a year.[11]

In extrajudicial appeals to the Holy See Pope Clement V

[7] C. 19, *de electione et electi potestate, I*, 6, in VI°.
[8] C. 41, *de electione et electi potestate, I*, 6, in VI°.
[9] C. 9, *de appellationibus*, II, 15, in VI°.
[10] C. 10, *de appellationibus*, II, 15, in VI°.
[11] C. 3, *de appellationibus*, II, 12, in Clem.

ordered that the appellant notify the appellee either personally (i.e. in the presence of the appellee or of his specially designated proxy) or through a signed document. If, however, the appellee was absent at the time and he had not appointed a proxy, a signed notice of the appeal was to be delivered to his home or to the Cathedral church, and in either case it was also to be made public in the church or benefice about which the appeal was concerned. But if this could not be done in view of the intimidation and dominance perpetrated by the appellee, then the notice of the appeal was to be made in a public place and with such solemnity that the appellee or his proxy would learn of it. Intimation of the appeal made in any other way lacked juridical effect. The pope expressly limited the application of this statute to appeals concerning elections.[12]

Pope Clement V added a further specification regarding the statute of Gregory X. He explained[13] that the statute applied only when in relation to the election the appeal raised a question regarding the criminal status of the elected person, or concerning some defect in form or procedure of the election. It did not apply when one directly prosecuted one's own right or the reputed right of a church.

The Council of Trent (1545-1563) ordered the appellant to present the acts of the court of first instance to the appellate tribunal. The appellant was to obtain these acts from the superior or judge from whose decree or sentence the appeal was made. A period of thirty days was granted to the judge to place the original acts at the disposal of the appellant for obtaining the needed copy.[14] Although this conciliar regulation was applied primarily to judicial appeal, it was applicable also to extrajudicial appeal because this latter was governed by the norms for its judicial counterpart.[15]

A decree of the Sacred Congregation of Bishops and

[12] C. 3, *de electione et electi potestate,* I, 3, in Clem.

[13] C. 4, *de electione et electi potestate,* I, 3, in Clem.

[14] Sess. XIII, *de ref.*, c. 3.

[15] Cf. Hostiensis, Lib. II, tit. *de appellationibus,* cap. 5, § 3; Panormitanus, tit. *de appellationibus,* (II, 51, 8).

Regulars, dated October 16, 1600,[16] insisted that appeals, both judicial and extrajudicial,[17] were to be received through an actual presentation of public documents to the superior tribunal. It had to be evident that an injury had been sustained.[18] The court which had pronounced the sentence was to give an authentic copy of the acts of the process to the appellant within a brief time.[19] The acts forwarded to the higher court had to contain a statement which revealed the tenor of the definitively rendered sentence.[20] The notary of the court of first instance was not obliged to send the original acts of the procedure to the appellate court, unless with reference to a copy some suspicion of falsification was justified on the side of the appellate court. If the original of the acts had been sent, they were to be returned to the ordinary for safekeeping in the archives of the court which had furnished them.[21]

When Pius X (1903-1914) completely reorganized the Roman Curia, he enacted some regulations in line with which the Sacred Congregations were to proceed in their consideration of extrajudicial cases.[22] He ordered that when non-judicial cases of an administrative or disciplinary character were brought before any of the Congregations, there was to be no joinder of issue, no hearing of witnesses, and no presentation of letters from sponsors (*nullis scriptis patronum receptis*). However, the parties concerned were to be heard, and the documents which they introduced were to be considered.[23] Those concerned in these administrative or dis-

[16] *Fontes*, n. 1586.

[17] It is evident that this decree was applicable to extrajudicial appeal because it contained references to extrajudicial matters, e.g., the decrees of the cleric who makes a canonical visitation—n. 7 of the cited decree.

[18] *Ibid.*, n. 3.

[19] *Ibid.*, n. 6.

[20] *Ibid.*, n. 5.

[21] *Ibid.*, n. 11.

[22] *Ordo Servandus in Romana Curia—Normae Peculiares—AAS*, I (1909), 59-108—hereinafter cited *Normae Peculiares*.

[23] *Normae Peculiares*, *cap.* III, art. 2, 7°—*AAS*, I (1909), 64-65.

ciplinary cases were to be notified either directly or through their ordinaries.[24]

If the parties wished to do so, they could have their written documents printed, but they had to observe the norm that a defense should cover not more than twenty pages and the response not more than ten pages.[25] If more pages were required, proper permission had to be requested beforehand.

B. *Present Discipline*

What procedure, according to the Code, is to be used in making a recourse? Generally the Code is silent on the procedure for recourse. In a few instances only does it set any requirements regarding the manner of proceeding in these extrajudicial cases.

a. *Making the Recourse*

It is necessary that a judicial appeal be initiated before the judge against whose sentence judicial redress is sought.[26] This norm does not seem to be applicable to recourse whether it operate with or without a suspensive effect. Dealing with the suspensive recourse of canon 647, the Sacred Congregation of Religious decreed that it could be interposed either directly by means of a letter sent to the Sacred Congregation, or mediately through the person who communicated the decree of dismissal to the religious.[27] And the Sacred Congregation of the Council held that, to receive the advantage of the secondary suspensive effect of the recourse which canon 2146 allows him, the removed pastor must notify the ordinary after he has interposed his recourse before the Sacred Congregation.[28] In both these decisions the Sacred Congregations imply that there is no necessity of initiating the recourse before the superior against whose action redress is sought.

These decisions of the Congregations are in accord with the policy of the Holy See that her offices are open to everyone

[24] *Ibid.*, 8°—*AAS*, I (1909), 65.

[25] *Ibid.*, 9°—*AAS*, I (1909), 65; *Lex Propria S. Romanae Rotae et Signaturae Apostolicae*, 29 iun. 1908, can. 29, § 1—*AAS*, I (1909), 27.

[26] Can. 1881.

[27] *Declaratio*, 20 iul. 1923—*AAS*, XV (1923), 457.

[28] *Romana et aliarum*, 14 ian. 1924—*AAS*, XVI (1924), 165.

of the faithful. "*Christi fideli cuique patet aditus ad Sanctae Sedis Officia, servata rite forma quae decet, et facultas est cum iisdem agendi per se de suis negotiis.*"[29] This statement of policy refers to the Congregations and Tribunals as well as to the Offices of the Roman Curia, since from the context it is evident that "*Officia*" has here a general meaning.

One may not argue by analogy from canon 1881 that recourses must be made in the presence of the authority against whom redress is sought. As Roberti points out,[30] the analogy between recourse and appeal is not a close one, and therefore one cannot accept the norm for appeal as the norm for recourse. Rather, recourse is to be ruled by its own norms.[31] Consequently, in the absence of any specific statement in the law one must conclude that there is no need of interposing the recourse before the superior against whom redress is sought.

Although no express prescript of the law demands that a recourse to Rome be made in writing, the custom of the Sacred Congregations is to decline the admission of oral petitions.[32] Usually an oral petition is less accurate and its precise import is all too easily forgotten. Likewise a recourse should not be made by telegram, since it seems that the letter of the Papal Secretary of State in 1891, which forbade the sending of petitions by telegraph, is still binding.[33] With the elimination of oral and telegraphic petitions it becomes evident that the only acceptable means of interposing a recourse is a letter.

Recourse is made simply by forwarding to the Holy See the petition in the form of a letter. Apparently, recourse may still be made through the agency of a proxy.

Must the ordinary or superior be notified that a recourse has been made? Here a distinction must be maintained be-

[29] *Normae Communes*, cap. X, sect. 1, 1°—*AAS*, I (1909), 53.

[30] "De recursu ob reiectionem libelli"—*Apollinaris*, (Romae, 1928—), I (1928), 73-74.

[31] *Apollinaris*, I (1928), 73, footnote 1.

[32] Wernz-Vidal, *Ius Canonicum*, V, 527, footnote 125.

[33] Secret. Stat., litt. 10 dec. 1891—*Collectanea S. Congregationis de Propaganda Fide* (2 vols., Romae, 1907), n. 1775—hereinafter cited *Collectanea*.

tween recourses according to the variable effect—suspensive and non-suspensive—that may attend them.

Monin states: "... *non jam, ut olim, ad S. Poenitentiariam, sed ad caetera quoque omnia Curiae dicasteria quisque potest directe et per se missis etiam epistolis recurrere, quin teneatur Ordinarii licentiam aut commendationem praeviam obtinere ...*"[34] He was speaking not of administrative recourse in particular, but of any pleas addressed to the Roman Congregations. However his words are applicable to recourse. There is no need of obtaining the permission or the commendation of the ordinary to make a recourse. The Code gave all the necessary permission when it established recourse as the means of redress in administrative and disciplinary matters.

There is, moreover, no legal requirement that the superior be notified after the recourse has been made, if that recourse does not operate with a suspensive effect. In pre-Code law there was no requirement of notifying the superior when a supplication was made, although it was required that notification be given in the cases of extrajudicial appeal. When the recourse is without a suspensive effect there is no reason for demanding that the superior be notified that a recourse has been made. His jurisdiction or dominative power remains unhampered. Furthermore, in all cases in which the superior has a justified interest he will be notified by the Sacred Congregations that the recourse has been taken.[35]

Although there is no requirement for validity, or even for licitness, that the superior be notified of a recourse taken against his decrees, precepts, directions, etc., this notification is nonetheless advisable, if a speedy disposition of the recourse is desired. The Holy See is not likely to revoke an episcopal decree or precept or direction without hearing the bishop's views on the case. The Congregations will, moreover, want to have in their possession certain data of the case which can be obtained from the bishop alone. If the party making the recourse notifies the bishop or the superior, either of the latter may then forward to Rome a statement of his views on the

[34] *De Curia Romana* (Lovanii: Van Linthout, 1912), p. 191.
[35] *Normae Peculiares*, cap. III, art. 2, 8°—*AAS*, I (1909), 65.

matter together with the required data. Thus, much time will be saved. Furthermore, it is a matter of equity and of respect that a subject notify his superior that he is referring the decree to the judgment of the Holy See.

On the other hand, it seems that the superior must be notified of the recourse that has been made to the Holy See when the recourse is such as to operate with a suspensive effect. Otherwise the superior would have no way of knowing that his decree, precept or direction no longer operates with binding power as it did before the recourse was made. He would learn of this important effect of the recourse only after some time, namely, when he receives a communication from Rome requesting him to transmit such acts and data as he may be able to furnish.

The grossly undisciplined results likely to follow from such a situation can easily be foreseen. If, for instance, the bishop has inflicted a vindicative penalty of suspension on one of his clerics, and the cleric thereupon makes a recourse to the Sacred Congregation of the Council, the continued force of the penalty is suspended.[36] The cleric accordingly may act as though no suspension was inflicted upon him. If the ordinary knew nothing about the recourse, he would feel duty-bound to take further measures to penalize the cleric who continues to exercise the functions of the priesthood, from which, as far as the bishop knows, he is suspended. Such a state of affairs would become very embarrassing for the authorities concerned. Therefore it seems that, when the law allows a recourse with suspensive effect, it presupposes that the ordinary or superior will be notified that his decree, precept, direction, etc. has been deprived of the efficacy it previously had.

This opinion of the writer seems supported by the fact that the Code always insists that some authentic notification be received by the party concerned before the revocation of his erstwhile power takes effect. Thus, delegated power is revoked through the direct intimation of this revocation to the one delegated,[37] and the one who resigns from an ecclesi-

[36] Can. 2287.

[37] Can. 207, § 1.

astical office continues as the incumbent in that office until he has received official notice that his resignation has been accepted.[38] The vicar general retains the powers of his office until he receives certain knowledge of the death of the bishop.[39] A removable incumbent when deprived of his office (even the parochial office) continues in its incumbency and with its powers until he has been notified by the superior concerning the act of deprivation.[40] Similarly, any power granted through a rescript[41] or a privilege,[42] when either of these latter are revoked by a special act (other than a law) of a superior, remains in force until the revocation of the rescript or privilege is made known to the one who had previously received them. In these cases the mind of the legislator was that the common good demanded that power remain in force until there is received some official notification of revocation. It seems, therefore, that we may argue from canon 20 that the ordinary or superior must be notified if a suspension in the efficacy of his enactments is to ensue with due effect.

This opinion of the writer receives further support from a study of the Resolution of the Congregation of the Council on the recourse of which canon 2146 makes mention.[43] The Congregation stated: *"Tempus utile ad recursum interponendum a definitivo decreto remotionis, ad effectum § 3 can. 2146 Codicis, esse decemdium ab intimatione eiusdem decreti . . . certiore facto Ordinario loci ab ipso recurrente de legitime interposito recursu ad Apostolicam Sedem."* The Congregation seems to insist on the notification of the ordinary, if the recourse is to have its specified effect. The need for the notification is evident; unless he is notified the ordinary would not know that he is bound by the norm of canon 2146, § 3, i.e. that he may not validly confer the parish on another cleric until the pastor's recourse has been settled. The writer has found no author who discusses the strength of the Congregation's

[38] Can. 190, § 2.
[39] Can. 430, § 2.
[40] Can. 192, § 3.
[41] Can. 60, § 1.
[42] Can. 71.
[43] *Romana et aliarum*, 14 ian. 1924—*AAS*, XVI (1924), 165.

demand that the ordinary be notified of the interposed recourse. It is clear that the observance of the requirement is not necessary for either the validity or merely the licitness of the recourse itself since the Resolution of the Congregation speaks of the recourse as having been "legitimately interposed."[44] The recourse of the pastor against the definitive decree of removal is valid and licit whether or not the ordinary is notified. The notification is demanded in regard to the effects of the recourse rather than in regard to the recourse itself. The wording of the Resolution of the Congregation implies that the notification of the ordinary is necessary for the valid application of the effects of the recourse, as stated in canon 2146, § 3. Consequently, it seems to the writer that, if the cleric fails to notify the ordinary that he has made the recourse, he may not claim the specified effects of the recourse.

When the ordinary is notified that a recourse with suspensive effect has been made, it is advisable that the notification be given in such a way that it can be legally proved in case any question about the validity of the suspensive effect of the recourse arises later. Consequently, if the notification is given orally, witnesses should be present; if it is sent to the ordinary by mail, a copy of the letter should be retained, the letter should be registered, and a return receipt requested in confirmation of its safely effected delivery.[45]

b. *The Letter of Recourse*

It has already been shown that the usual means of making a recourse is a letter.[46]

The letter should be typewritten, or at least written in a legible style. Good, white paper should be used, and the typing or writing should be on only one side of the paper. The recourse proper should be addressed to the Holy Father himself, starting with the salutation "*Beatissime Pater*". To speed

[44] "*legitime interposito recursu.*"

[45] S.C. de Religiosis, declar. 20 iul. 1923, ad 2: "Ad interpositi recursus probationem requiritur et sufficit vel authenticum documentum vel saltem duorum fide dignorum hominum testimonium."—*AAS*, XV (1923), 457.

[46] Cf. *supra*, p. 37.

the consideration of the recourse, the letter should be written in one of the languages of the Roman Curia, viz. Latin, French or Italian. Clerics, especially ecclesiastical dignitaries, should always use Latin, the official language of the Church, in their correspondence with the Holy See.[47]

If the person making a recourse is unfamiliar with the languages of the Roman Curia, he may write in English, Spanish, German or Portuguese, since Pius X ordered each Sacred Congregation to have auditors who were conversant with at least one of these tongues.[48] But this will delay the disposition of the recourse until the letter has been translated into a language with which the Consultors are familiar. If it happens that a person still cannot express himself in one of the above-mentioned tongues, he may compose the letter in whatever language he knows. However, it would be better if he would obtain the services of someone who knows one of the Curial languages to compose the letter for him; then he could sign the letter and forward it to Rome.

The letter should be brief, clear and to the point. It should give only those matters which are necessary for an understanding of the point on which the recourse insists. It should contain the full name of the person making the recourse, his ecclesiastical status (priest, deacon, religious, layman, etc.), his place of residence and his diocese or religious community. Then in a lucid manner the matter of the recourse should be given; the decree or precept or penalty etc. should be stated; the superior who gave the decree or precept or penalty etc. should be named together with his ecclesiastical office, his place of residence and his diocese or religious community.

Furthermore, there should be some indication of the way in which the party making the recourse is subject to this superior, i.e. through domicile, quasi-domicile, religious profession, etc. The reasons for the recourse should be set forth completely, showing why the party regards the decree or precept or penalty, etc., as unjust and injurious, or at least detrimental to his rights or interest. If the person making the re-

[47] Cf. Cappello, *De Curia Romana* (2 vols., Romae, 1911), I, 44.

[48] *Normae Peculiares*, Cap. VI, 5°—AAS, I (1909), 73.

course seeks reparation for any damage which may have come to him as a result of his superior's action, he should make this clear in his letter. The party must be most careful to state the unblemished truth, for a discovered untruth will naturally place his entire recourse under suspicion. The date of the writing should be affixed, and the letter signed by the party.

c. *The Acts and Data*

In administrative recourse the acts and data which attend the case are called *acta negotii* in opposition to the *acta causae* of a judicial appeal.[49]

Usually the documents which are sent to Rome are not the originals. An authentic copy suffices[50] unless there is room for suspicion of falsification in the copy, in which case the originals should be forwarded with due precautions to insure their safe delivery.[51] If the originals are sent, an authentic copy should be kept in the diocesan archives. The copies sent to the Holy See should bear a certification regarding the accurate and integral transcription of the acts and data, and should carry the signature of the diocesan curia's notary or chancellor.[52]

This certification of the transcription may be made with the usual rubber stamp, widely used by diocesan curias for imprinting the words "*Concordat cum originali*". It would be best that each page of the copy bear this imprint of certification. Moreover, if the original document has been translated into one of the languages of the Roman Curia, the copy should reveal a certification regarding the accuracy of the translation (*testificatio de fidelitate versionis*), and this certification should be vouched for by the signature either of the

[49] Noval, *De Processibus*, II, n. 512. The *acta negotii* may be designated as the "data construed in the plea," and the *acta causae* as the "judicial acts of the trial."

[50] Cf. cans. 1644, § 1, and 1890 where this principle is stated in the case of judicial appeal.

[51] Cf. S.C. Ep. et Reg., decr. 16 oct. 1600, n. 11—*Fontes*, n. 1586; can. 1644, § 1.

[52] Cf. can. 1644, § 1; Capello, *Praxis Processualis* (Taurini, Marietti, 1940), n. 197.

curia's notary or of the diocesan chancellor.[53] It seems that today photostatic copies of the original acts will be accepted by the Sacred Congregations.[54]

The acts or data should be sent to the Holy See by the ordinary or the superior. Noval[55] argues from canon 1890[56] that the superior or ordinary should on his own initiative forward the documents to Rome. Whether or not this norm needs to be applied when recourse is made, it is undeniable that it would be prudent for the ordinary or superior to send the documents as soon as he learns of the recourse; if he does not forward them voluntarily, the Holy See will demand that he send them. It is clear from canon 2146, § 2,[57] and from canon 2194[58] that the ordinary has an obligation to forward all the acts and data of the administrative processes mentioned in canons 2147 to 2194. This seems to be a grave obligation in justice.[59] The ordinary should forward the acts and data within a brief period of time after the party notified him that a recourse has been made. There seems to be no reason why with reference to every recourse this norm should not be regarded as a law which has been enacted in matters of like import and concern (*lex lata in similibus*) and that therefore ordinaries and superiors are obliged to transmit all pertinent documents to the Sacred Congregations when a recourse is made.

[53] Cappello, *Praxis Processualis*, n. 197.

[54] "If photostatic copies are made with the proper precautions and under the surveillance of the local Ordinary, it appears that they should be accorded the same degree of credence as written transcripts."—Doheny, *Canonical Procedure in Matrimonial Cases* (Milwaukee, Bruce Publishing Co., 1938), p. 282.

[55] *De Processibus*, II, n. 512.

[56] "Interposita appellatione tribunal a quo debet ad iudicem ad quem actorum causae authenticum exemplar vel ipsamet originalia acta causae transmittere . . ."

[57] "Quo in casu ad Sanctam Sedem omnia acta processus transmittenda sunt."

[58] "Si clericus recursum a suspensione sibi inflicta interponat, Ordinarius ad Sedem Apostolicam mittere debet probationes quibus constet clericum revera perpetrasse quod extraordinaria hac poena puniri queat."

[59] Cf. Meier, *Penal Administrative Procedure against Negligent Pastors*, p. 205.

What documents compose the acts and data in connection with a recourse? In general, all documents pertinent to the decree, precept, penalty, direction, etc., and to the alleged injustice or detriment to right or interest comprise the data construed in the plea (*acta negotii*). In each recourse the required documents will be different.

If the recourse is made against a decree or a precept, the superior should send to Rome an authentic copy of the decree or the precept. If the decree or precept was given orally before two witnesses and was never put in written form, he should restate it as clearly and exactly as he can recall it after consulting the witnesses who heard it imposed. It would help the Sacred Congregation to reach a decision if the superior stated the circumstances of and the reasons for giving the decree or precept. If the superior does not state these circumstances and reasons when he forwards the acts and data, the Sacred Congregation will in all probability delay the settlement of the recourse until it has contacted him and has thus given him an opportunity to present his side of the dispute.[60] The superior must forward to Rome whatever proof is necessary to show the justice of his decree or precept.

If the recourse is made against a penalty, whether medicinal or vindicative, the superior who imposed the penalty must prove that the party committed the crime, and that the crime was sufficiently grave to call for the inflicted penalty. Moreover, when the penalty is a censure, he must show that contumacy was present in the delinquency; if the censure was of a *ferendae sententiae* character, then proof must be given that the monitions and warnings were given and disregarded.[61]

When a recourse is made against the definitive decree of the administrative processes mentioned in canons 2147 to 2185, the ordinary must transmit to the Holy See all the acts of the process ("*omnia acta processus*").[62] Evidently, in this pas-

[60] Suarez, *De Remotione Parochorum*, n. 20; Reilly, *Residence of Pastors*, The Catholic University of America Canon Law Studies, n. 97 (Washington, D. C.: The Catholic University of America, 1935) p. 67; Noval, *De Processibus*, II, n. 512.

[61] Can. 2242, § 2.

[62] Can. 2146, § 2.

sage of canon 2146, § 2, the Code does not use the phrase *"acta processus"* in the same sense as it uses it in canon 1642, § 1, where it designates the formalities of judicial procedure, e.g. the citations, intimations, etc., in contrast to the *"acta causae,"* which comprise the judicial acts of the trial, such as the recorded proofs and the formulated sentence. In canon 2146 the phrase has a wider meaning; its concept there embraces all the acts transpiring in the official procedure, whether they are concerned with the merits of the case or with the formalities.[63] The *"omnia acta processus"* should therefore include everything from the first admonition to the definitive decree. It should include such formalities as the recorded appointment of the notaries and of the examiners and the parish priest consultors, the record of their oaths of secrecy, and the written report of the issued invitations and intimated admonitions. It embraces, too, the recorded proofs accompanying the accusation, the registered replies of the party, the transcribed testimony of witnesses etc. and copies of the issued decrees, since without all these the Holy See would be unable to reach a just and equitable decision in the case. This opinion is uncontestable, for usually a recourse is made not in view of an omitted formality, but in view of an allegedly committed injustice in fact.[64] Thus, the *"omnia acta processus"* in connection with the making of a recourse include also the *acta causae* as strictly considered in relation to a judicial trial.

If in consequence of a definitive decree an irremovable pastor was removed from office, the acts and data connected with the recourse should include a record of the proof that the pastor was invited to resign,[65] of the proof that a serious cause motivated this invitation, of the replies of the pastor, of the final appraisal (*votum*) furnished by the two examiners, of the testimony of any witnesses who may have been called, then, also, a copy of the first decree, a record of the recourse made

[63] Coronata, *Institutiones*, III, n. 1578; Cf. Suarez, *De Remotione Parochorum*, n. 22; Noval, *De Processibus*, II, n. 456; Reilly, *Residence of Pastors*, p. 67; Meier, *Penal Administrative Procedure against Negligent Pastors*, p. 204.

[64] Suarez, *De Remotione Parochorum*, n. 22.

[65] Can. 2148, § 1.

against this decree, a transcript of the new evidence adduced by the pastor, a written report of the final appraisal submitted by the two parish priest consultors, and, ultimately, a copy of the definitive decree.[66]

When the pastor is a removable incumbent, the acts and data should consist of documents revealing proof of the existence of a just and grave cause for action on the part of the ordinary, and of the fact that an invitation to resign was extended to the pastor. They should likewise contain a written record of the pastor's reply, a transcript of the final appraisal furnished by the two examiners, a notation of the repeated exhortation to resign coupled with the threat of removal if the pastor failed to submit his resignation within the specified time limit, and a copy of the decree of removal issued by the ordinary when the specified limit of time had elapsed without the pastor's compliance with the order to resign his pastoral office.

In a recourse against the transfer of a removable pastor, the ordinary should send to the Holy See a record of his proof that the good of souls required the transfer, and that he requested the pastor to agree to the transfer; the ordinary should also send a transcript of the reply of the pastor, and of the final appraisal of the two parish priest consultors; and, finally, the ordinary should furnish a description of the two parishes involved in the act of transfer, a copy of the exhortation that the pastor submit to the will of the ordinary, a transcript of the reply of the pastor to this exhortation, of the ordinary's command to accept the new parish within the specified limit of time, of his indication that the parish from which the transfer was to be made would be declared vacant at the end of that time-limit, and a facsimile of the decree which then declared the parish vacant.

The data construed in a plea of recourse by a pastor, a beneficiary, or a cleric who has been removed from office because of non-residence should include written mention of the warning to observe the law of residence and, if no answer was given to this warning and the incumbent did not resume his

[66] Cf. Vermeersch-Creusen, *Epitome*, III, n. 346, 2°.

residence, then a copy of the decree of deprivation. The acts of the recourse should furthermore contain a copy of the reply of the cleric if he did answer the warning, a transcript of the final appraisal of the examiners, of the investigations, of the second warning to resume residence within the specified limit of time and a facsimile of the decree of deprivation of the removable pastor who did not comply with the intent of this second warning. If the pastor was irremovable, then in addition to the documents just mentioned there should be forwarded a copy of his reply to the second warning, of the final appraisal of the examiners, of the new investigations, of the decree of the ordinary commanding him to resume residence within the specified limit of time under penalty of being *ipso facto* removed from his benefice, and a facsimile of the decree declaring the benefice vacant.

In the case of a cleric who has maintained forbidden residence with a woman of suspect character the acts of the recourse include, besides a record of the proof of the accusation lodged against him, the notation of the ordinary's warning coupled with the threat of penalties, the record of the cleric's reply or the mention of his failure to reply, and the written designation of the inflicted penalty. If the cleric is a removable pastor and replies to the warning of the ordinary, the acts of the recourse should reveal a record of the excuses he offers, of the final appraisal furnished by the examiners, of the formal imposition of the precept, of the disregard of the precept, and of the issuance of the decree of deprivation. If the pastor is irremovable, there should be in addition a record of the replies of the pastor to the precept, of the examiner's final appraisal, of the repetition of the precept, and of the inflicted penalty.

When a pastor is penalized because of pastoral negligence, the acts should contain a notation of proof concerning his negligence, a mention of the warning issued by the ordinary, written advertence to the lack of amendment on the part of the pastor, to the opportunity offered him for defense, to the elements of his defense or the fact of his silence, to the examiners' final appraisal, and to the inflicted penalty. If further neglect has continued, then in the case of a removable pastor there must likewise be included in the acts of the recourse a record of his deprivation of office; in the case of an irremovable pastor, a notation of the inflicted withholding of beneficial income, and in the event of subsequent non-amendment, a record of the submitted proofs concerning this non-compliance, and of the ultimately issued decree of deprivation.

When recourse is invoked against a suspension inflicted by the ordinary in view of his private but reliable knowledge (*ex informata conscientia*) that a serious occult delict has been perpetrated by a cleric, then the acts of the recourse must contain a record of the submitted proof that a delict was really committed, that it was of a grossly reprehensible character, and that apart from serious detriment and untoward consequences the ordinary had no other available means for proceeding against the cleric.[67] When the recourse is made, the acts must advert to these three points, and the record must reveal what proofs were at hand for justifying the infliction of this extraordinary penalty. The ordinary must, moreover, forward a copy of the decree of suspension to the Sacred Congregation of the Council in the case of a diocesan cleric,[68] and to the Sacred Congregation for Religious in the case of a cleric who is a member of some religious institute or community.[69]

The acts for the recourse of a religious in temporary vows against a decree of dismissal should reveal the gravity of the cause for dismissal, the fact that these causes were manifested to the religious, the matter of his reply, the content of his submitted proofs and the wording of the decree of dismissal. When the religious is in perpetual vows, there should be a record of the submitted proof regarding the three external and grave delicts, a notation of the twice repeated warnings, mention of the incorrigibility of the religious, a statement regarding the opportunity of the religious to defend himself, a record of the replies of the religious and a copy of the decree issued by the ordinary or by the supreme moderator.[70]

In every other recourse the general principles demon-

[67] Can. 2194; Suarez, *De Remotione Parochorum*, n. 255.

[68] Cf. can. 250, § 1.

[69] Cf. can. 251, § 1.

[70] Schaefer, *De Religiosis*, n. 522, d.

strated above should be followed. There should be shown the reasons for the superior's decree, act or disposition: this postulates in the acts of the recourse a recounting of the proofs which the superior can submit in substantiation of the rightful issuance of his authoritative act. There should likewise be shown the reasons on which the counterplea is based: this demands that in the acts of the recourse there be a statement of the proofs regarding the alleged injury to his rights or detriment to his interests which the subject can adduce in furtherance of his claims.

CHAPTER IV

TIME-LIMIT FOR MAKING A RECOURSE

A. *Presence or Absence of a Time-Limit*

By the word "*terminus*" canonists understand that determined period of time during which a certain act must be placed or completed.[1] These fixed periods of time may be of a legal, of a judicial, or of a conventional character.[2] They are called legal in character when the time period is determined by law; judicial when it is set by a judge after he has consulted the parties in a case; and conventional when with the approval of the judge the parties agree upon a time-limit. In the present chapter there is question simply of the time periods set by law.

The time periods fixed by the law of the Code are all of a peremptory nature,[3] and accordingly are in Latin referred to as *fatalia*. Once the pre-determined period of time has passed, the legal act may no longer be initiated. The fixed time-limits (*fatalia*) are granted for a definite purpose, as for the use of the right of appeal; but the use of that right is temporally conditioned within a fixed limit. Any appeal which is lodged outside the fixed time limits stands automatically annulled, for it has failed to comply with a condition on which its legal force depends.[4]

The fixed time limit within which an appeal can be lodged is the ten days following the notification of the publication of the sentence.[5] However, there is no canon which determines in a general way the limit of time within which a recourse must be made. Nevertheless, there are several canons which state a fixed time-limit for recourses in particular matters. These canons may be divided into three groups:

A. The patron of a church, or also his presentee, is al-

[1] "Fatalia . . . id est termini perimendis iuribus . . . constituti."—Can. 1634, § 1.

[2] Can. 1634, §§ 1-2.

[3] Can. 1634, § 1.

[4] Can. 1886; Roberti, *De Processibus*, I, n. 180; Wernz-Vidal, *Ius Canonicum*, IV, nn. 185 and 610.

[5] Can. 1881.

lowed ten days within which to make a recourse to the Holy See against the decision of the ordinary that the presentee is not a fit prospective incumbent in the office or benefice which the patron intended he should possess.[6] An irremovable pastor is granted ten days in which to initiate his recourse to the ordinary against the first decree of removal.[7]

B. A recourse to the superior tribunal against the declaration of the judge that he is incompetent to hear a case must be made within ten days.[8] When a judge rejects a bill of complaint (*libellus*), the recourse may be made to the superior tribunal within ten days.[9]

C. If one with the right of suffrage in an ecclesiastical election was not called to the election and consequently was absent, he must avail himself of the possible recourse within three days from the reception of notification that the election has taken place.[10]

Since the publication of the Code, the Roman Congregations have, with the approval of the Holy Father, set a fixed time-limit for two cases of recourse. The Congregation of Religious has declared that the time for a religious in temporary vows to make a recourse with suspensive effect against a decree of dismissal in ten days.[11] A similar ten day period was made the norm for a recourse, *"ad effectum § 3, can. 2146 Codicis,"* undertaken by a pastor against the definitive decree of removal in the administrative process.[12]

[6] Can. 1465, § 1.

[7] Can. 2153, § 1. In this case, as we shall show in the next chapter, there is not a true recourse, since it is made not to a higher authority but to the same authority who issued the decree of removal.

[8] Can. 1610, § 3.

[9] Can. 1709, § 3.

[10] Can. 162, § 2.

[11] S. C. de Religiosis, 20 iul. 1923: "Tempus utile ad interponendum recursum quoad effectum suspensivum, de quo in can. 647, § 2, esse decem dierum ab intimatione decreti religioso dimisso facta, iuxta normam traditam in similibus casibus, ut can. 1465, § 1 et can. 2155, § 1, 2 (sic—2153, § 1)."—AAS, XV (1923), 457; Bouscaren, C.L.D., I, 328.

[12] S.C.C., *Romana et aliarum,* 14 ian. 1924: "Tempus utile ad recursum interponendum a definitivo decreto remotionis, ad effectum § 3 can. 2146 Codicis, esse decemdium ab intimatione eiusdem decreti, supputandum

These declarations of the Sacred Congregations are not authentic interpretations of the canons in question, since the power of giving authentic interpretations is reserved to the Commission for the Interpretation of the Canons of the Code.[13] They are rather general declaratory interpretations given in accord with the power conceded to the Sacred Congregations by Benedict XV (1914-1922).[14]

Only in the above-mentioned cases is there expressly indicated a legal time-limit within which a recourse must be made. Are these cases examples of the general norm, or are they exceptions?

Some light is thrown on the whole matter when one studies the cases in which a time limit is fixed. In the first group noted above and in the canons dealt with by the Congregations,[15] the recourses have either a suspensive effect, or a non-suspensive effect which however, in the cases under consideration, is coupled with a suspension of the ordinary's power to confer a benefice or a parish. These suspensive or partially suspensive effects of the recourses are the reasons for the time-limit.[16]

Since these recourses are at least partially *in suspensivo*, the ordinary would not feel free in his administration until the recourse had been settled. The dismissed religious might notify the superior that he intends to make a recourse, and then delay for a long time the actual making of the recourse, meanwhile demanding to be regarded as a religious because of the suspensive effect of the recourse. The removed pastor might

ad normam can. 34, § 3, 3°, et can. 35; certiore facto ordinario loci ab ipso recurrente de legitime interposito recursu ad Apostolicam Sedem."—*AAS*, XVI (1924), 165; Bouscaren, *C.L.D.*, I, 837.

[13] Benedictus XV, motu propr. *Cum Iuris Canonici Codicem*, 15 sept. 1917, n. 1—*AAS*, IX (1917), 483.

[14] Motu propr. *Cum Iuris Canonici Codicem*, 15 sept. 1917, n. 2: "Ordinarium igitur earum munus in hoc genere erit tum curare ut Codicis praescripta religiose serventur, tum *Instructiones* . . . edere, quae iisdem Codicis praeceptis maiorem et lucem afferant et efficientiam pariant."—*AAS*, IX (1917), 483.

[15] Cans. 1465, § 1; 2153, § 1; and 647, § 2, 4°; 2146, §§ 1-2.

[16] Cf. S. C. C., *Romana et aliarum*, 14 ian. 1924, *Animadversiones*—*AAS*, XVI (1924), 163-165; "Annotationes", *Periodica*, XII (1923), 101; Noval, *De Processibus*, II, n. 509; Sipos, *Enchiridion*, p. 859.

do likewise, and his ordinary would be unable to appoint a new pastor until the Holy See had decided the case. Thus true justice could be frustrated and the administration of the religious superior or of the local ordinary would be impeded. The Church could not allow such dilatory tactics to obstruct justice. So she sets a time-limit for these recourses, "lest what is granted in defense of justice become converted to a remedy and assignment for iniquity."[17] Thus she obviates interference with the course of justice.

The *Animadversiones* to the reply of the Sacred Congregation of the Council concerning canon 2146, § 1, argued that, since the recourses mentioned in canons 1465, § 1, and 2153, § 1, are *in suspensivo,* they partake more of the nature of appeal than of supplication. *"Nimirium cum ordinario recursus meriti examen quin provisionem suspendat, quoties contrarium accidit, appellationis regulas sequi debet . . ."*[18] The *Animadversiones* concluded that the same time-limit that governed appeals[19] should govern recourses which operate with suspensive effects.

The Sacred Congregation of Religious used the same criterion[20] in determining the time-limit for the available recourse which is mentioned in canon 647. In its declaration this Congregation, relying on canon 20, stated that the norm was to be taken from canons 1465, § 1, and 2153, § 1, which it considered as laws enacted in matters of like import (*"leges latas in similibus"*).

For these cases, therefore, one may rightfully assume that the Church set fixed limits of time for the use of these recourses because of the suspensive effects that attend their operation.

The canons of the second group[21] deal with matters that

[17] S.C.C., *Romana et aliarum, Animadversiones*: ". . . ne quod in iustitiae praesidium conceditur, in iniquitatis fomentum traducatur"—AAS, XVI (1924), 164.

[18] *Loc. cit.*

[19] Can. 1881.

[20] Maroto, "Annotationes", *Commentarium pro Religiosis* (Romae, 1920—), (ab anno 1935: *Commentarium pro Religiosis et Missionariis*), IV (1923), 356.

[21] Cans. 1610, § 3, and 1709, § 3.

pertain to the judicial power, viz. the declaration of incompetence and the rejection of a bill of complaint. The remedy in these cases so closely approaches judicial appeal that in canon 1610, § 3, the Code actually speaks of it as appeal,[22] whereas it is actually a matter for recourse, since it deals with an extrajudicial or administrative act of a judge. Similarity with appeal derives from the requirement that the recourse is made to the superior tribunal, the *iudex ad quem* in cases of judicial appeal.[23]

It seems that this similarity with appeal furnishes the reason for the fixed time-limit in these cases. The time-limit set in these cases seems to constitute positive legislation enacted for particular instances. It does not seem that the *Animadversiones* of the Sacred Congregation of the Council presented a correct statement when it was mentioned that a time-limit was set for the recourse which canon 1709, § 3, allows, because the recourse operated with a suspensive effect. An attentive reading of the paragraph of the canon[24] fails to indicate to this writer a suspensive effect for the recourse. The decision of the judge that he lacks competence is not suspended, since there is no reason to believe that after this recourse the judge may proceed as though he were competent. His decision retains its force until it is reversed by the higher judge.

Canon 162, § 2, deals with the recourse invoked by an elector against an election at which he was not present because of lack of notification. The canon indicates a time-limit of three days for his optional recourse. Under pre-Code law this was a case for extrajudicial appeal, and accordingly was governed by the ten-day restrictive time-limit. Moreover, if, in such an election, even one elector has been contemptuously excluded, the election was to be declared invalid.[25]

[22] ". . . potest . . . appellationem ad superius tribunal interponere."

[23] Can. 1594, § 1.

[24] "Adversus libelli reiectionem integum semper est parti intra tempus utile decem dierum recursum interponere ad superius tribunal a quo, audita parte, et promotore iustitiae aut vinculi defensore quaestio reiectionis expeditissime definienda est."

[25] Cc. 28, 36, 55, X, *de electione et electi potestate,* I, 6; S.C.C. *Ortonen.*, 29 maii 1852—*Fontes*, n. 4123.

Under the present discipline the election is valid, but the competent superior must nullify it at the insistence of one who has rightfully used his option of recourse against it and has, moreover, succeeded in proving the point which warranted his use of the recourse. The advisability of a fixed time-limit in this case is evident. If no such temporal restriction were set, a validly elected superior might be removed from office at any time because of the recourse of an elector, who possibly through no fault of the new superior, had not been called to the election. That the time-limit here is an example of legislation for a particular case is made evident by the specific duration of the allotted time; here the time-limit is not the usual ten days, but a period of only three days, which determination is peculiar to this recourse. The recourse in this case bears a resemblance to a rescissory judicial action or suit which aims at the revocation of valid contracts in which a party was fraudulently circumvented.[26]

In each case in which a time-limit is set for the invoking of a recourse, either by the Code or by a Roman Congregation, there is, then, a special reason or need for the time-limit, namely, either the suspensive effect of the recourse, or the similarity to appeal, or the prescript of positive legislation. Noval well says:

> "... *praescriptum Codicis quoad tempus utile decemdii pro recursibus contemplatis in dictis tribus canonibus* [1465, § 1, 1709, 2153, § 1] *non fuit latum eo quod sint recursus, sed quia sunt recursus speciales, seu ob quandam rationem eis propriam, et proinde non potest extendi, vi regulae c.* 20, *ad omnes recursus, sed tantum ad eos in quibus illa specialis ratio inveniatur.*"[27]

There can be no doubt that the recourses for which the option of use is restricted within a set limit of time do not exemplify a norm which applies generally for all options of recourse. The specific mention of a time-limit in these particular cases argues strongly that no such time-limit is set in

[26] Can. 1684.

[27] *De Processibus*, II, n. 509.

the usual case of recourse. If a time-limit were specified for every option of recourse, there would be no necessity of mentioning the time-limit in particular cases.

Free option for recourse in general, that is, independence of a restricted time-limit, is implied by the declarations of the Sacred Congregations of Religious and the Sacred Congregation of the Council. The declarations stated that the ten-day time-limit was applicable to a recourse *"quoad effectum suspensivum"*[28] or *"ad effectum § 3, can. 2146 Codicis."*[29] They set no time-limit on the optional use of recourse which operates with only a non-suspensive effect. The latter kind of recourse may be invoked at any time, even after the ten days have elapsed.[30]

When the recourse has only a non-suspensive effect the superior or ordinary is not hindered in his administration by the possibility of the suspension of his power or jurisdiction in the matter through any suspensive operation of the recourse; he does not have to wait until some set time-limit has elapsed before he can proceed with the case. His decree takes effect immediately. So, there is no need for a time-limit, either from the viewpoint of the superior or ordinary or from the viewpoint of the one who is making the recourse. The superior or ordinary knows that his decree or precept has taken effect, and so he may urge obedience to it immediately. The subject knows that he is free at any time to take his recourse to the Holy See.

It was always the characteristic of a supplication that its use was not conditioned within narrow temporal limits.[31] It is true that the Codex of Justinian set a two-year time-limit for the use of a supplication, but it is evident from the wording of the law that it was concerned with a supplication against a judicial sentence.[32] This provision of Roman Law was ap-

[28] S.C. de Religiosis, 20 iul. 1923—*AAS*, XV (1923), 457.

[29] S.C.C., *Romana et aliarum*, 14 ian. 1924—*AAS*, XVI (1924), 165.

[30] Maroto, "Annotationes", *Commentarium pro Religiosis*, IV (1923), 356.

[31] Suarez, *De Remotione Parochorum*, n. 21.

[32] C. (7. 42) un.: "Litigantibus in amplissimo praetorianae praefecturae iudicio, si contra ius se laesos adfirment, non provocandi, sed

plied by canonists to supplication as an extraordinary remedy against a judicial sentence.[33] The more general norm, however, was the one mentioned by the Rota when it stated: "*Cum ad Principem supremum recursus numquam interdictus censeatur a quo quemadmodum iurisdictiones fluunt, ita etiam conveniens est ut postea refluant.*"[34] Actually the Roman Congregations have accepted recourses a long time after the injury has been inflicted.[35]

Pre-Code law did, however, set a time-limit for extrajudicial appeals. According to the Roman Law,[36] which Gratian incorporated in his *Decretum,*[37] ten days was the usual time allowed for making a judicial appeal. Since extrajudicial appeal was governed in non-odious matters by the norms for its judicial counterpart,[38] a ten-day time-limit was set for its use. These ten days were counted from the time when the injury was suffered, and they were computed as a *tempus utile,* that is, as long as one was without an opportunity to make an appeal, there was no lapse of time in one's disfavor.[39]

Boniface VIII confirmed this ten-day limitation of the time for lodging an appeal against an extrajudicial act. These ten days began to lapse as soon as the injured party realized

supplicandi licentiam ministramus, licet pro curia vel qualibet publica utilitate seu alia causa dicatur prolata sententia (nec enim publice prodest singulis legum adminicula denegari): ita videlicet, ut intra biennium tantum nostro numini contra cognitionales sedis praetorianae praefecturae sententias, post successionem iudicis numerandum, supplicandi eis tribuatur facultas."

[33] Cf. *Glossa Ordinaria* s. v. *supplicavit* in c. 4, X, *de in integrum restitutione,* I, 41; Reiffenstuel, Lib. II, tit. 28, n. 20.

[34] S.R.R., *Cracovien.,* 31 ian. 1676, nn. 22 & 23—*Sacrae Rotae Romanae Decisiones Recentiores,* ed. Farinaccius, Rubeus et Compagnus (25 vols., Venetiis et Romae, 1673-1697), Vol. XVIII, pars. 2., dec. 639, p. 393.

[35] Cf. S.C.C., *Concordien.,* 20 feb. 1897—*Fontes,* n. 4300. Here the Congregation stated that recourse, and not appeal, could be invoked in a particular case in which an injury had been inflicted on February 16, 1895.

[36] N. (23. 1, 2, 3, 4).

[37] Cf. c. 28, C. II, q. 6.

[38] Panormitanus, tit. *de appellationibus,* (II, 51, 8); Hostiensis, Lib. II, tit. *de appellationibus,* cap. 5, § 3; Pirhing, Lib. II, tit. 28, n. 3.

[39] D. (49, 4) 1, § *Biduum;* c. 29, C. II, q. 6.

that he had cause for appeal. After the ten days had passed, an appeal in these extrajudicial matters was not to be heard.[40] However, even upon the expiration of this fixed duration of time the injured party could still make a supplication.

As we noted in the first chapter, extrajudicial appeal is no longer a canonical institution. Consequently, the time-limit to which it was held is no longer applicable to recourse.

The Church has always stressed the fact that the Roman See is a haven of protection for its children. Over it rules the Vicar of Christ whom they may approach not only for guidance, but even for defense against unjust actions.[41] Any member of the clergy or of the laity is free, according to the teaching of the Church, to approach at any time the Roman Pontiff with a request for justice,[42] for the Sovereign Pontiff's jurisdiction is ordinary and immediate in regard to every member of the Church.[43]

This freedom or right of the faithful should not be limited unless legislation expressly curtails it. Such a curtailment is found, for example, in the time-limit set by the law for the lodging of a judicial appeal, but even after the time-limit for appeal has passed, the person may approach the Pope through

[40] "Statuimus ut ab electionibus, provisionibus et quibuslibet extraiudicialibus actibus, in quibus potest appellatio interponi, quisquis ex eis, gravatum se reputans, per appellationis beneficium gravamen illatum desideraverit revocari, intra decem dies, postquam sciverit, si velit, appellet; post decendium vero eidem aditus non pateat appellandi."—c. 8, *de appellationibus*, II, 15, in VI°.

[41] *Concilium Sardicen.*, cc. 3, 4, and 5—Hardouin, *Acta Conciliorum et Epistolae Decretales ac Constitutiones Summorum Pontificum* (12 vols., Parisiis, 1714-1715), I, 324—hereinafter cited Hardouin; cc. 4, 5, 6, 8, C. II, q. 6; *Conc. Vat.*, Sess. IV, *De Constitutione Ecclesiae*, cap. 3—Mansi, LII, 1332 and Denzinger-Bannwart-Umberg, *Enchiridion Symbolorum, Definitionum, et Declarationum de Rebus Fidei et Morum* (21-23 ed., Friburgi Brisgoviae: Herder & Co., 1937), n. 1830—hereinafter cited Denzinger-Bannwart-Umberg; S.C. de Prop Fide, instr. 20 oct. 1881, n. 12—*Collectanea*, n. 1628; *Normae Communes*, Cap. X, sec. 1, 1°—*AAS*, I (1909), 53; can. 1569, § 1.

[42] *Conc. Vat.*, sess. IV, *De Constitutione Ecclesiae*, cap. 3—Mansi, LII, 1332; Denzinger-Bannwart-Umberg, n. 1830.

[43] Can. 218, § 2; *Conc. Vat.*, sess. IV, *De Constitutione Ecclesiae*, cap. 3, canon un.—Mansi, LII, 1333; Denzinger-Bannwart-Umberg, n. 1831.

a supplication. The purpose of this particular curtailment is to preserve appeal as an aid for the innocent, and to prevent it from becoming a dilatory tactic on the part of the guilty. Since appeal operates with suspensive effect, the legislator feared that unprincipled parties would delay the lodging of the appeal to prevent the execution of the sentence, and hence he felt that the public welfare demanded that a time-limit be placed on the introduction of an appeal. Since there is no such legislation with reference to recourse, one must conclude that freedom is in possession, and that therefore there is no specified time-limit for the making of a recourse unless the law ordains otherwise in particular cases.

Moreover, compliance with the demand which is inherent in the fixed time-limit is binding not only on the party who makes an appeal or a recourse but also on the judge or the superior.[44] It would certainly be incorrect to say that any law which is merely ecclesiastical so binds the Roman Pontiff that he may not receive from his subjects a recourse which operates simply with a non-suspensive effect. Such a statement could not be reconciled with the supreme and full power of jurisdiction which the Pope possesses.[45]

It may now be asked whether a predetermined and fixed time-limit is established with reference to a recourse which is made against inflicted vindicative penalties. Such a recourse has, as a rule, a suspensive effect.[46] There has been no authentic statement on this matter. However, canon 20 states that, when in a certain matter an express prescript of the law is lacking, the norm is to be borrowed from such laws as have been enacted in similar matters. The *"leges latae in similibus"* with reference to the question of recourse against inflicted vindicative penalties are canons 647, § 2, 4°, 1465, § 1, 2146 and 2153, § 1—all of which deal with recourses that operate with a fully suspensive or at least partially suspensive effect,

[44] Suarez, *De Remotione Parochorum*, n. 21; Murphy, *Suspension ex Informata Conscientia*, The Catholic University of American Canon Law Studies, n. 76 (Washington, D. C.: The Catholic University of America, 1932), p. 117.

[45] Can. 218, § 1.

[46] Can. 2287.

and all of which can be invoked only within the indicated time-limit of ten days in order to receive the suspensive effect. The Sacred Congregation of Religious expressly stated that this was its mode of procedure in establishing the norm for the available time-limit in connection with the recourse mentioned in canon 647, § 2, 4°.[47]

The norm is to be taken from these canons rather than, as Murphy suggests,[48] from canon 1889, § 1, since this latter canon deals with an appeal, whereas the former canons deal with a recourse that operates with a suspensive effect.[49] However, canon 1889, § 1, may be used as a secondary argument in this question, since there is a marked similarity between appeals and recourses with suspensive effect. One may, therefore, conclude that a recourse from an inflicted vindicative penalty must be invoked with the ten-day time-limit, if it is to have a suspensive effect. In this matter, as in all other matters, a recourse may still be made even after the ten days have elapsed, but in that event the recourse will not operate with a suspensive effect.

B. Available Time (*Tempus Utile*)

It must now be considered whether the ten-day period which is fixed as a time-limit for the effective use of certain recourses which are attended with a suspensive effect is to be considered as a *tempus utile* or as a *tempus continuum*, that is, does the period allow an interruption when some obstacle occurs, or does it run continually and without interruption regardless of any accompanying obstacle.

The Code defines these terms as follows: "*Tempus* UTILE *illud intelligitur quod pro exercitio aut prosecutione sui iuris ita alicui competit ut ignoranti aut agere non valenti non currat;* CONTINUUM, *quod nullum patitur interruptionem.*"[50]

Tempus continuum connotes the progression and duration of time in the way in which it is ordinarily reckoned. Thus

[47] S.C. de Religiosis, 20 iul. 1923: ". . . iuxta norman traditam in similibus casibus, ut can. 1465, § 1, et 2155, § 1" (N.B. the Congregation actually meant can. 2153, § 1)—*AAS*, XV (1923), 457.

[48] *Suspension ex Informata Conscientia*, p. 118.

[49] Cf. Noval, *De Processibus*, II, n. 509.

[50] Can. 35.

the *tempus continuum* of a calendar month connotes, for example, the lapse of time from June 1st to July 1st. It denotes an unbroken succession which in the lapse of time abstracts from all interruptions. The computed lapse of time remains unaffected by the obstacles which prevent a person from executing or prosecuting his rights. An example of *tempus continuum* is furnished in canon 1710. If a judge has not acted upon a bill of complaint within a month after it was presented, the interested party can insist that the judge perform his task; if nevertheless the judge remains inactive, the party can, upon the lapse of five days from his previous insistence, interpose a recourse with the local ordinary, provided that he is not the acting judge, or with the higher tribunal in order either to constrain the judge to implement a definition of the judicial cause, or to have someone else supplant him for achieving the same task.[51] The periods here mentioned, the month and the five days, are to be computed in the nature of an uninterrupted duration of time (*tempus continuum*).[52]

Tempus utile, or available time, points rather to an exceptional method of reckoning time. As a juridic institute it comes to us practically unchanged from Roman Law.[53] When the lapse of time is computed only according as the time is available for use, there arises for the interested party a distinct advantage. If any hindrance, for which he is not responsible, prevents him from prosecuting or using his rights, then the allotted available time will not lapse until that hindrance has been obviated. If, for example, some attending impediment has lasted for three days, then an equal number of days must be added if the specifically allotted time is to reach its completion. If a *dies feriatus*[54] occurs within or at the end of a *tempus utile*, this day is not to be computed in judicial cases

[51] The recourse in this case is not the administrative recourse with which this paper is concerned. It is rather a "judicial" recourse.

[52] Cf. Coronata, *Institutiones*, III, n. 1238, 3°.

[53] D. (38. 15); D. (44. 3) 1; D. (48. 50) 12 [11] 5.

[54] Can. 1639, § 1, states that all feasts of precept and also the last three days of Holy Week are *dies feriati*, that is days on which all court procedure normally is precluded.

as a day of possible court action.[55] It is possible that an impediment will arise after five of the ten days have passed. In such a case the remaining five days are not counted until the impediment has ceased.[56]

Only two classes of obstacles can actually delay or interrupt the passage of time in a period which is set as a *tempus utile*, viz., ignorance or inability to act.[57] The ignorance can exist in relation either to the possession of the right itself, or to the perpetrated violation of that right by another.[58] This ignorance, if it is legitimately and effectively to exist as a hindrance, cannot allowedly be crass or supine in character. It must be such as normally befalls a person who exercises at least an ordinary prudence and interest in the usual responsibilities of life.[59] If an adult rational person is ignorant of a fact which is known to everyone else, he none-the-less suffers the loss of his rights which he failed to prosecute in consequence of such ignorance.[60]

The inability to act may be physical or legal. It is physical when sickness, lack of transportation, etc. prevents the use or prosecution of a right. It is legal when excommunication,

[55] Can. 1635.

[56] De Meester, *Compendium*, III, n. 1748; Vermeersch-Creusen, *Epitome*, III, n. 454, 3, 3°; Beste, *Introductio*, p. 105; Dubé, *The General Principles for the Reckoning of Time in Canon Law*, The Catholic University of America Canon Law Studies, n. 144 (Washington, D. C.: The Catholic University of America Press, 1941), p. 241—hereinafter cited *Reckoning of Time;* Christ, *Dispensation from Vindicative Penalties*, The Catholic University of America Canon Law Studies, n. 174 (Washington, D. C.: The Catholic University of America Press, 1943), p. 213.

[57] Can. 35.

[58] *Glossa Ordinaria* s. v. *sciverit* in c. 8, *de appellationibus*, II, 15, in VI°; Augustine, *A Commentary on the New Code of Canon Law* (7. ed., 8 vols., St. Louis: B. Herder Co., 1943), I, 123; Dubé, *Reckoning of Time*, p. 231.

[59] Van Hove, *Commentarium Lovaniense in Codicem Iuris Canonici*, Vol. III *De Temporis Supputatione* (Mechliniae: H. Dessain, 1933), n. 320—hereinafter cited as *De Temporis Supputatione;* Cicognani, *Canon Law*, Authorized English Version by the Rev. Joseph M. O'Hara, Ph.D., and the Rev. Francis Brennan, D.D., J.U.D. (Philadelphia: The Dolphin Press, 1935), p. 693; Michiels, *Normae Generales*, II, 158.

[60] ". . . si quis quod omnibus perspectum est ignoret, sui iuris amissionem sibi imputare debet".—Toso, *Commentaria Minora*, I, 113.

suspension, etc. prevent this use or prosecution. In cases of recourse excommunication or suspension will not contitute any inability to act, for the recourse is often concerned with these very penalties.[61]

The Code expressly states in only one case that recourse is to be made within ten days computable as *tempus utile,* viz., when it allows recourse against the rejection of a bill of complaint.[62]

The Sacred Congregations expressly state that ten days is the time available (*tempus utile*) for the interposition of the recourse of a dismissed religious in temporary vows in so far as the suspensive effect of the recourse is to remain intact,[63] and of the recourse of a pastor against a definitive decree of removal for the safeguarding of the effect of paragraph 3 of canon 2146.[64] However, some doubt may arise in reference to the exact significance of the phrase "*tempus utile*" in the declarations of the Sacred Congregations. Do the Congregations mean that the time at the party's avail is ten days or do they mean that the ten days are constituted as a period of *tempus utile*? In other words, do the Congregations mean that the days between the issuance of the decree and the notification of the party are not to be counted but after the notification the period of ten days is to be regarded as *tempus continuum,* or do they mean that even after the notification the ten days are to be regarded as *tempus utile?*

The writer feels that the Congregations used the phrase in the latter sense, viz., that even after the notification has been received the party has ten available days in which to make his recourse. His reasons for this conclusion are the

[61] Cf. cans. 2243 and 2287.

[62] Can. 1709, § 3. Cf. Dubé, *Reckoning of Time,* p. 235.

[63] S.C. de Religiosis, 20 iul. 1923: "Tempus utile ad interponendum recursum quoad effectum suspensivum, de quo in canone 647, § 2, esse decem dierum ab intimatione decreti religioso dimisso facta"—*AAS,* XV (1923), 457.

[64] S.C.C., *Romana et aliarum,* 14 ian. 1924: "Tempus utile ad recursum interponendum a definitivo decreto remotionis, ad effectum § 3, can. 2146 Codicis, esse decemdium ab intimatione eiusdem decreti, supputandum ad norman can. 34, § 3, 3°, et can. 35."—*AAS,* XVI (1924), 165.

the following. The declaration of the Congregation of the Council expressly states that the ten-day period of time is to be computed according to the norms of canons 34, § 3, 3°, and 35. An instruction which the Congregation of Religious appended to its declaration says: "The available time of ten days from notice of the decree given to the religious is to be computed according to the norm of canon 34, § 3, 3°, and, according to the dispositions of canon 35, so that it does not run if the dismissed party is ignorant of his right to make recourse or is unable to do so . . ."[65] The reference to canon 34 regards the computation of the starting point of the ten days, i.e., if the time of the notification does not coincide with the beginning of a day, that day is not to be counted. The reference to canon 35 regards the computation of the specific ten days of available time, i.e., "that is understood as available time which so belongs to anyone for the exercise or prosecution of his right that it does not run for one who is ignorant or who cannot act."[66]

Can it be argued from these responses that when the recourse has a suspensive effect, the time allowed for the making of a recourse is always to be computed as available time? It seems perfectly right to argue to such a conclusion. In reaching their decisions that the recourses mentioned in canon 647, § 2, 4°, and in canon 2146, § 3, must be made within ten days to enjoy the advantage of the suspensive or partially suspensive effects indicated in these canons, the Sacred Congregations argued from the norm of canons 1465, § 1, and 2153, § 1, and other similar canons. It should be equally valid to argue the other way around, viz., from the norm of canons 647, § 2, 4°, and 2146, § 3, to the norm for similar canons. Thus the recourses which operate with suspensive or partially suspen-

[65] S.C. de Religiosis, decl. 20 iul. 1923: "3°. Tempus utile decem dierum ab intimatione decreti Religioso facta supputandum erit ad normam can. 34, § 3, n. 3°, et ita ut non currat si dimissus recurrendi ius ignoret aut agere non valeat iuxta dispositiones can. 35 . . ."—*AAS*, XV (1923), 457-458.

[66] Can. 35: "Tempus *utile* illud intelligitur quod pro exercitio aut prosecutione sui iuris ita alicui competit ut ignoranti aut agere non valenti non currat. . . ."

sive effects could be made within a ten day period of *tempus utile,* just as the extrajudical appeals in the pre-Code law were invoked.[67]

The use of the *tempus utile* seems applicable in the recourse of a patron, or of his presentee, against the rejection of that presentee by the ordinary,[68] in the recourse against inflicted vindicative penalties,[69] in the recourse against precepts threatening the infliction of censures when the precept deals with a matter in which a suspensive effect is granted to the recourse,[70] and in any other recourse to which the law grants a suspensive effect.

Since the time in these recourses is to be computed as a *tempus utile,* ignorance either of his right to invoke the recourse or of the injury that has been done to him does not occasion any forfeiture of a person's option to avail himself of a recourse with suspensive effect. If, for example, a religious in temporary vows does not learn until fifteen days after he has received notification of the decree of dismissal that he has the right to make a recourse against the decree, he still has ten full days in which to make the recourse with its operative suspensive effect, for the time that is such that it stands at one's avail does not lapse when one is ignorant of possessing it, or of having a right which can be exercised while one possesses it.[71] Again, it could happen that a removable pastor who has been transferred against his wishes, but according to the norms of canons 2162 to 2167, knows that he has the right to make a recourse, but he does not realize that the parish to which he has been assigned is quite inferior to the one from which he was transferred. In this case the period of the *tempus utile* allotted for the making of the recourse will begin to lapse only when he realizes the inferiority of the new parish.

Incapacity to act does not prejudice the right of a person to make a recourse with suspensive effect.[72] In cases of re-

[67] C. 29, C. II, q. 6.
[68] Can. 1465, § 1.
[69] Can. 2287.
[70] Can. 2243, § 2.
[71] "Tempus utile . . . ignoranti . . . non currat."—Can. 35.
[72] "Tempus utile . . . agere non valenti non currat."—Can. 35.

course there will be question of physical incapacity only, since recourse may be had even though a person has been excommunicated or suspended.[73] This physical incapacity may be personal to the one who makes the recourse, or it may be extraneous to him and yet prevent the making of the recourse. If a religious in temporary vows had become so seriously ill after receiving a decree of dismissal that he was unable to make the recourse mentioned in canon 647, the period of time during which he was so incapacitated would not be included in the ten day period of the *tempus utile*.[74] However, he must be really incapacitated by the sickness, not merely inconvenienced. The sickness must make the recourse really difficult and not merely irksome. If the person is well enough to write an ordinary friendly letter, he should be considered usually well enough to write the letter required for a recourse.

Another case of physical incapacity is that of a person who lives in a remote district where communication facilities are not available for long periods; such a person would be unable to send his recourse to the Holy See within the allotted period of time. It would be wise for him to write his letter within the specified time-limit, and then forward the letter at the first opportunity. It seems necessary that such a person make known in some way within the specified time his intention of making a recourse, if he wishes to take advantage of the suspensive effects attaching to his recourse when made within the proper allotted period of time. Otherwise a suspicion could arise that he was using circumstances to frustrate the aim of the decree or precept. He should make known his intention in some form which later will serve to establish proof of the fact of his incapacity to make the recourse at the expected time. He can do this either in writing or orally before two witnesses.

If a person is ignorant or incapacitated for only some portion of a day, is that day to be counted in the ten days

[73] Cf. cans. 2194; 2243, §§ 1-2; 2287.

[74] Cf. Reilly, *Residence of Pastors*, p. 66; Meier, *Penal Administrative Procedure against Negligent Pastors*, p. 202. In these works analogous cases are discussed by the authors.

allowed for the recourse? Authors say[75] that if a person is thus impeded for a notable part of a day, the day is not to be computed as constituting any part of the *tempus utile.*

What constitutes a "notable part of a day"? Authors are not too clear in this regard. Since one must eat and sleep, a good part of each day is impeded in these ways alone. But it is evident that the authors do not consider the "notable part of a day" in the light of these human necessities. Rather, when they speak of a day, they have in mind the amount of time that one may actually use for the assertion of his rights.

Kealy[76] and Dubé[77] say that the higher authority to whom the appeal or recourse is made is the one to decide whether or not the time during which one was impeded constituted a notable part of a day. Dubé says:[78]

> "It [the determination of what constitutes a notable part of a day] depends, first of all, on the nature of the institute involved, but simultaneously also on a limited number of accompanying circumstances which a prudent judge or superior must consider and weigh in determining whether or not this or that day is to be considered as being juridically of no avail."

What Kealy and Dubé say is doubtlessly true, but it does not help the person who plans to make a recourse in deciding whether or not he has an extra day in which to do so, and still reap the benefit of the suspensive effect inherent in a timely made recourse.

Kealy[79] recounts a further opinion. It offers a tangible

[75] "Qui per maiorem diei partem impeditus fuerit, per integrum diem impeditus existimatur."—Cappello, *Summa Iuris Canonici,* I, n. 182; cf. Van Hove, *De Temporis Supputatione,* n. 321; Coronata, *Institutiones,* I, n. 56, 3; Wernz-Vidal, *Ius Canonicum,* I, n. 251; Vermeersch-Creusen, *Epitome,* I, n. 121; Dubé, *Reckoning of Time,* p. 237.

[76] *The Introductory Libellus in Church Court Procedure,* The Catholic University of America Canon Law Studies, n. 108 (Washington, D. C.: The Catholic University of America, 1937), p. 70—hereinafter cited Introductory Libellus.

[77] *Reckoning of Time,* p. 239.

[78] *Loc. cit.*

[79] *Introductory Libellus,* p. 70.

norm in accordance with which a person may settle his own doubts before the matter goes to the superior.

> "A stricter opinion is that in view of the ease with which recourse may be made any solid opportunity for so doing during the day should be counted against the agent; and if he allows the day to pass without using his opportunity the day should not be regarded as impeded even though he may have been hindered during several hours of the day. One who holds this opinion might argue that a person occupied for six or eight hours in the day and unoccupied for the remainder of his waking hours has had sufficient opportunity to have recourse on that day and, hence, the day should be counted as one of the ten days allowed by the law."

This opinion seems to the writer to be the correct one. The purpose of the fixed time-limit for the making of a recourse is to limit a person's right to suspend the effects of a decree, precept, etc. when the recourse is granted a suspensive effect. If a person has sufficient opportunity during a day to make his recourse and does not take advantage of the opportunity, it certainly is not inequitable to consider the day as forfeited. No one needs ten or twelve hours to make a recourse, since it does not take an ordinary person that long to write a letter. Usually an hour or two suffices. If a person has that much leisure time during his waking hours and fails to use it for the making of the recourse, he should be regarded as having lost the day. If some such limit is not placed on the interpretation of what constitutes a day available for the making of the recourse, it seems to this writer not at all unlikely that there would occur instances in which the ten day period of *tempus utile* could run on indefinitely.

The *tempus utile* begins after the person has learned of the decree, the precept, etc. in some official way.[80] A mere

[80] ". . . intra decem dies a significatione recusationis . . ."—Can. 1465, § 1: S.C. de Religiosis, 20 iul. 1923: ". . . decem dierum ab intimatione decreti religioso dismisso facta . . ."—*AAS*, XV (1923), 457; S.C.C., *Romana et aliarum*, 14 ian. 1924: ". . . decemdium ab intimationis eiusdem decreti [amotionis] . . ."—*AAS*, XVI (1924), 165.

rumor or unofficial report that a superior or an ordinary is going to issue a decree or precept is not sufficient as notification. In judicial matters the time for appeal is not computed until some authentic information of the sentence has been given to the party.[81] This information in judicial matters is given either by citing the party to hear the sentence, or by posting the sentence on the bulletin board of the tribunal, so that everyone may read it, or by sending a copy of the sentence to the parties by registered mail.[82] It seems warranted to maintain that the party in a recourse must obtain his knowledge of the decree, precept, etc. in a similar way. The period of *tempus utile* within which he is granted the option of making a recourse with suspensive effect begins after he has received this notification.

This notification is not likely to be received at the precise hour of midnight. Therefore, the ten days will not start until the following day in accord with the norm of canon 34, §3, 3°, which states: "If the starting point does not coincide with the beginning of the day . . . then the initial day is not to be counted."[83] Thus, if the notification is received on the first day of June, the ten days will start on the second day of June, and will end at midnight between the eleventh and twelfth of June.[84]

If a *dies feriatus* occurs on the last of the ten days allowed for a recourse with suspensive effect, may the party take advantage of this day and delay the making of his recourse until the next day, thus having eleven days? The reply must be in the negative. What is forbidden on a *dies feriatus* is any forensic act.[85] Under the name of forensic acts come

[81] "Appellatio interponi debet . . . intra decem dies a notitia publicationis sententiae."—Can. 1881. Cf. Connolly, *Appeals*, The Catholic University of America Canon Law Studies, n. 79 (Washington, D. C.: The Catholic University of America, 1932), p. 108.

[82] Can. 1877.

[83] Cf. S.C.C., *Romana et aliarum*, 14 ian. 1924—*AAS*, XVI (1924), 165; Cicognani, *Canon Law*, p. 689; Ayrinhac, *General Legislation in the New Code of Canon Law* (New York: Longmans, Green & Co., 1933), n. 127 c—hereinafter cited as General Legislation.

[84] Cf. Connolly, *Appeals*, p. 107; Dubé, *Reckoning of Time*, p. 236.

[85] Beste, *Introductio*, p. 780.

sessions of the court, trials, various formal judicial proceedings such as the citation of witnesses and the pronouncing of sentences, but not acts of a semi-private nature that require no strict judicial formalities.[86] Voluntary jurisdiction is not concerned with forensic acts, and so may be exercised even on a *dies feriatus*.[87] Consequently in the matter of a recourse a *dies feriatus* will not interfere with the conclusion of the ten day period of the *tempus utile*.[88]

Finally, it must be noted that although recourse with suspensive effect may not be made after the ten day period of *tempus utile* has elapsed, a person may still make a recourse, but in that event the recourse will not operate with the suspensive effect.[89]

[86] Can. 1639, § 1. Cf. Ayrinhac, *Administrative Legislation in the New Code of Canon Law* (New York: Longmans, Green & Co., 1930), n. 90, 3, 2°—hereinafter cited as Administrative Legislation.

[87] Vermeesch-Creusen, *Epitome*, II, n. 560; Sipos, *Enchiridion*, p. 654, footnote 12.

[88] Suarez, *De Remotione Parochorum*, n. 21.

[89] Maroto, "Annotationes"—*Commentarium pro Religiosis*, IV (1923), 355; Rainer, *Suspension of Clerics*, The Catholic University of America Canon Law Studies, n. 111 (Washington, D. C.: The Catholic University of America, 1937), p. 166; Meier, *Penal Administrative Procedure against Negligent Pastors*, p. 201; O'Neill, *The Dismissal of Religious in Temporary Vows*, The Catholic University of America Canon Law Studies, n. 166 (Washington, D. C.: The Catholic University of America Press, 1942), p. 166.

CHAPTER V

THE SUPERIOR *AD QUEM*

A. *Pre-Code Discipline.*

In pre-Code canonical parlance the authority to whom an appeal or supplication was made was called the *iudex ad quem* to distinguish between this superior and the one from whom the appeal or supplication was made. The latter was called the *iudex a quo.*

Since in pre-Code law extrajudicial appeal was governed by the norms for its judicial counterpart,[1] the *iudex ad quem* for an extrajudicial appeal from the administrative acts of an ordinary was the same superior who received judicial appeals from the tribunal of that ordinary.[2]

In the early centuries of the Church various local councils stipulated that the synod was the ordinary court of appeals, and the Ecumenical Council of Nicea in 325 ordered that synods be held twice yearly to hear the appeals of those who were under the sentence of excommunication.[3] Recognition of the synod as the court of appeal is to be found in the acts of the I Council of Vaison in Gaul in 442,[4] of the III Council of Orleans in 538,[5] and of the Synod of Rheims in about the year 625.[6]

Gradually the right of the metropolitan to receive appeals was being conceded by law. The Ecumenical Council of Chalcedon (451) allowed appeal to the metropolitan in certain ex-

[1] ". . . provocationes iure appellationis censeantur."—Hostiensis, Lib. I, tit. *de appellationibus*, cap. 5, § 3; "Haec bene nota ut in dispositionibus odiosis non comprehendatur appellatio extraiudicialis sub nomine appellationis."—Panormitanus, tit. *de appellationibus* (II, 51, 8).

[2] "Et haec Provocatio extrajudicialis debet fieri ad Judicem ordinarium, coram quo citandus, et vocandus esset Adversarius pro lite, dum est litigandum via ordinaria."—Fermosinus, VIII (*De Exceptionibus*), 392.

[3] Canon 5—Hardouin, I, 324.

[4] Canon 5—Bruns, *Canones Apostolorum et Conciliorum Veterum Selecti* (2 vols., Berolini, 1839), II, 128—hereinafter cited Bruns; Mansi, VI, 454.

[5] Canon 20—Bruns, II, 198; Mansi, IX, 17.

[6] Canon 5—Bruns, II, 261; Mansi, X, 594.

trajudicial matters; from the metropolitan the appeal was to be made to the primate, and from the primate to the patriarch.[7] The metropolitan was recognized by the V Council of Orleans in 549 as the *iudex ad quem* in disputes between a bishop and one of his clerics.[8] He was regarded as representing the court of second instance by the III Provincial Council of Toledo in 589,[9] by the XIII National Council of Toledo in 683,[10] and by the Council of Frankfurt in 794.[11]

By the time of Gratian the accepted procedure seems to have been that which was outlined by canon 17 of the Council of Chalcedon. Consequently, Gratian included in his *Decretum* a pseudo-Isidorian text which he wrongly ascribed to Pope Anacletus (76-88).[12] The *casus* to this canon of the *Decretum* explained that an appeal should be made from a minor prelate to a bishop, and from the bishop to the metropolitan; if the matter was not definitely decided before the metropolitan, or if the appellant suffered some injury at that tribunal, the appeal should be addressed to a council over which the patriarch or primate presided, and in which ecclesiastical major issues were considered. Thus, the *iudex ad quem* always had to hold an office higher than that of the *iudex a quo*.

The Council of Trent (1545-1563) prescribed that an appeal in criminal matters was to be made from the bishop or

[7] Canon 17—Bruns, I, 30; Mansi, VII, 389. This canon and the other 27 canons of the Council of Chalcedon were rejected by Pope Leo I (440-461) because they confirmed the secondary primacy of the Patriarch of Constantinople, and because they were formulated in the absence of the Papal Legates. Cf. Cicognani, *Canon Law*, p. 156; Funk, *A Manual of Church History*, trans. from 5. German ed. (2 vols., St. Louis: Herder & Co., 1910), I, 183-184.

[8] Canon 17—Bruns, II, 212; Mansi, IX, 133.

[9] Canon 20—Bruns, I, 218; Mansi, IX, 998.

[10] Cap. 12—Bruns, I, 346; Mansi, XI, 1074.

[11] Canon 6—Hardouin, IV, 905.

[12] "Omnis oppressus libere sacerdotum (si voluerit) appellet iudicium et a nullo prohibeatur: sed ab his fulciatur et liberetur et audiatur. Si autem difficiles causae aut maiora negotia orta fuerint, ad maiorem sedem referantur. Et si illic facile discerni non potuerint aut iuste terminari, ubi fuerit summorum congregata congregatio . . . iuste et Deo placite coram patriarcha aut primate ecclesiastica negotia et coram patricio seculari iudicentur negotia in commune."—c. 3, C. II, q. 6—Jaffé, n. 2.

his vicar general to the metropolitan.[13] However, if the metropolitan was suspect, or if he resided more than two legal days' journey away, then the appeal might be made to one of the neighboring bishops. But the judge of the appeal was never to be of a lower rank than was the judge of the first instance.

During all these centuries of legislation on appeal, the right of an ultimate appeal to the Sovereign Pontiff was always recognized.[14] The right of the Holy See to receive such appeals was inherent in its supremacy of jurisdiction in the Church.

As was previously stated, supplication in the restricted sense was always addressed to the Holy See. Since this supplication or recourse was a plea that the *iudex ad quem* use his sovereign powers in favor of the petitioner, it had by its very nature to be addressed to the sovereign of the Church, the Roman Pontiff.

B. *Present Discipline*

According to the norms of the Code of Canon Law, the metropolitan is not competent to receive an appeal from any extrajudicial act of his suffragan bishops. Although he is still the competent authority to receive judicial appeals from suffragan dioceses,[15] he may no longer receive a remonstrance against the decrees of ordinaries.[16] Similarly, patriarchs and primates have no authority to sit in judgement on the extrajudicial decrees and precepts of ordinaries.[17] Recourse is now entirely an administrative process, and no longer adopts its norms from the laws on judicial appeal. Metropolitans, patriarchs and primates have no extrajudicial authority over

[13] Sess. XXII, *de ref.*, c. 7—Schroeder, *Canons and Decrees of the Council of Trent* (St. Louis: Herder & Co., 1941), pp. 156 and 428—hereinafter cited Schroeder.

[14] Cf. cc. 4, 5, 6, 8, C. II, q. 6; Jaffé, nn. 183, 299, 323, 80; Pius IV, const. *De salute gregis*, 4 sept. 1560—*Fontes*, n. 98.

[15] Cans. 274, 7°; 1594, § 1.

[16] Can. 1601.

[17] Cf. can. 271.

their suffragan dioceses,[18] unless some law confers this right upon them.[19]

The only ecclesiastical person who has authority over the extrajudicial acts of ordinaries is the Roman Pontiff. According to the Code[20] the Holy Father has supreme and full jurisdiction in the Church Universal, not only in matters of faith and morals, but even in matters pertaining to the discipline and government of the Church in every part of the world. His power is ordinary and immediate in regard to each and every church, and in regard to each and every member of the faithful, whether he be bishop, priest or layman.[21]

The Pope's authority over each bishop and diocese is such that each ordinary must every five years give to him a detailed account of the state of the diocese and of his administration of it.[22] Moreover, he is the supreme administrator and dispenser of all ecclesiastical goods,[23] and has the right to confer a benefice in any diocese on whomsoever he chooses, and to reserve to himself the conferral of any benefice in any diocese.[24] He alone is the competent judge in all cases of Cardinals,[25] Legates of the Apostolic See, and in criminal matters Bishops.[26] He has, consequently, the right to review the decisions of ordinaries and religious superiors in both judicial and non-judicial matters.

Since the Church has such a widespread and numerous membership, it would be impossible for any one man to direct every detail of Church business. Consequently, the Roman Pontiffs have established the Sacred Congregations, Tribunals

[18] Metropolitans have a devolved power in the two cases mentioned in can. 274, 1°, and 5°, when the suffragan has neglected his duties, and in can. 432, § 2, when the Cathedral Chapter has failed to appoint an administrator of the diocese within the time allotted after the diocese has become vacant.

[19] Cf. cans. 1610, § 3; 1709, § 3; 1710.

[20] Can. 218, § 1.

[21] Can. 218, § 2.

[22] Can. 340, § 1.

[23] Can. 1518.

[24] Can. 1431.

[25] Can. 1557, § 1, 2°.

[26] Can. 1557, § 1, 3°.

and Offices of the Roman Curia to assist them in the stupendous task of governing the Church Universal. The Congregations, Tribunals and Offices act in the name and by the authority of the Holy Father. Their powers are ordinary (but vicarious), supreme and universal within their proper spheres, unless some express provision rules to the contrary.[27]

Most judicial matters are reserved to the Tribunals.[28] The competency of the Offices is of a ministerial nature,[29] e.g. preparing and forwarding documents. The Congregations, which hold the principle place in the Roman Curia, are the ordinary channels through which the Popes exercise their executive and administrative powers.[30] The jurisdiction of each Congregation, Tribunal and Office is accurately determined as to matter, territory, persons and rite.[31]

According to the present law the Sacred Congregations have an exclusive right to receive recourses against the decrees issued by ordinaries.[32] According to the first constituted President of the Code Commission the force of this law extends to all administrative "decrees, acts and dispositions" of ordinaries.[33] Canon 1601 and the interpretation given to it by the Code Commission definitely removes recourse from the jurisdiction of any judicial tribunal.

Recourses, then, are dealt with by the Roman Congregations only, unless the law makes an exception in some particu-

[27] Cappello, *Summa Iuris Canonici*, I, n. 318, 3.

[28] Cans. 258-259.

[29] Cappello, *Summa Iuris Canonici*, I, n. 318; Beste, *Introductio*, p. 237.

[30] Ayrinhac, *Constitution of the Church in the New Code of Canon Law* (New York: Longmans, Green and Co., 1930), n. 37—hereinafter cited Constitution of the Church; Cappello, *loc. cit.*; Beste, *Introductio*, p. 237.

[31] Cans. 246-264.

[32] "Contra Ordinariorum decreta non datur appellatio seu recursus ad Sacram Rotam; sed de eiusmodi recursibus exclusive cognoscunt Sacrae Congregationes."—Can. 1601.

[33] "Mens est: exclusive competere Sacris Congregationibus cognitionem tum huiusmodi decretorum, actuum, dispositionum, tum damnorum quae quis praetendat ex iis sibi illata esse."—Praeses P.C.I.C., *dubia soluta*, 22 maii 1923—AAS, XVI (1924), 251; Bouscaren, *C.L.D.*, I, 739.

lar case. When a recourse is made, it will be sent to the Congregation which is competent in the matter. Most recourses will come under the competency of the Congregation of the Council, the Congregation of Religious, the Congregation for the Propagation of the Faith, and the Congregation for the Oriental Church.

To the Sacred Congregation of the Council are committed all matters referring to the universal discipline of the secular clergy and of the Christian people.[34] This is the Congregation competent to receive the recourses of the diocesan clerics from all legislative, executive and administrative decrees, acts and dispositions of their local ordinaries.[35] It is also competent to receive the recourses of lay persons in matters that come under its power. Within the ambit of its competency come pastors and canons, pious sodalities and unions (even though they depend upon religious societies or are erected in the churches or houses of religious), pious legacies and works, Mass stipends, benefices and offices, ecclesiastical goods, taxes of the episcopal Curia, and other similar matters.[36]

To this Congregation is reserved the faculty to dispense from conditions required for the acquisition of benefices (e.g. the determined age, the specified academic degree, etc.) whose conferral depends on the ordinary. The Congregation of the Council may also admit a compromise with persons who have obtained possession of ecclesiastical goods (even though these belonged to religious), and may allow the faithful to acquire ecclesiastical goods which have been usurped by the civil power.[37] It watches over ecclesiastical immunity and settles controversies on precedence, except in those questions of precedence which come under the competency of the Congregation of Religious or of the Ceremonial Congregation.[38] The Congregation of the Council, outside of the territories subject to the

[34] Can. 250, § 1.

[35] "Est autem haec Congregatio competens in omnibus controversiis negotia eidem commissa spectantibus, quas in linea disciplinari pertractandas censuerit."—Can. 250, § 5.

[36] Can. 250, § 2.

[37] Can. 250, § 2.

[38] Can. 250, § 3.

Congregation for the Propagation of the Faith, has charge of all things relative to the celebration and approval of councils and gatherings or conferences of bishops.[39]

A special Commission of Cardinals, appointed by the Pope according to the norm of canon 245 to settle controversies about the competence of the various Sacred Congregations, decided that the Congregation of the Council was competent to settle questions relating to priests as students or teachers in lay schools, and to associations of the clergy and to all federations of such associations.[40]

If the right of any diocesan cleric or layman has been injured in any of these matters, the injured party should take his recourse to the Sacred Congregation of the Council.[41] Consequently, it is to this Congregation that a member of the clergy will make his recourse against the ordinary's action in revoking the cleric's license to preach,[42] and from the ordinary's decree of uniting, transferring, dividing or dismembering a parish.[43] To it should be made the recourse of either diocesan cleric or layman against censures inflicted by a precept, or against a precept threatening the infliction of a censure not yet contracted,[44] and the recourse against vindicative penalties.[45]

The Sacred Congregation for the Affairs of Religious has exclusive authority over the government, discipline, studies, goods and privileges of religious.[46] Its competency includes the religious of either sex with either solemn or simple vows. It is the proper Congregation for persons without vows who live in common like religious, and for secular Third Orders as

[39] Can. 250, § 4.

[40] Coetus Cardinalium peculiariter designatus, 7 dec. 1922, n. 3—*AAS*, XV (1923), 39; Bouscaren, *C.L.D.*, I, 160.

[41] Can. 250, § 5; Pius X, const. *Sapienti Consilio*, 29 iun. 1908, art. 1, n. 4, 4—*AAS*, I (1909), 11; *Fontes*, n. 682.

[42] Can. 1340, § 3.

[43] Can. 1428, § 3.

[44] Can. 2243, §§ 1-2.

[45] Can. 2287.

[46] Can. 251, § 1.

such (not in matters in which the tertiaries as laymen are subject to their local ordinaries).[47]

If a dispute develops between a religious and one who is not a religious on the matter in which this Congregation is competent, this Sacred Congregation is the proper authority to which the dispute should be referred.[48] In such a case the Congregation may remit the matter to another Congregation.

The Sacred Congregation of Religious, then, is exclusively competent to receive all recourses which affect the rights or interests of any religious family or of any religious as such.[49] To it a religious will make his recourse against a decree of dismissal;[50] against censures inflicted or threatened by a religious ordinary;[51] against remedial penalties inflicted by a superior;[52] against vindicative penalties;[53] against the decrees of authorities in their canonical visitations;[54] and against the local ordinary's decrees, precepts or penalties which affect him as a religious.[55]

One must stress the fact that this Congregation is competent in matters which affect the religious as such. Cappello states[56] that when a question of ecclesiastical goods, offices, benefices, immunities, etc. directly affects a person as a religious, he makes his recourse to the Sacred Congregation of Religious; but when any similar question affects him as a religious only indirectly, he must address his recourse to the Congregation of the Council. Thus, a religious who is a pastor, makes his recourse to the Sacred Congregation of the Council against the division of his parish,[57] or against an assessment imposed on the parish by the bishop. In these and in similar

[47] Cf. Ayrinhac, *Constitution of the Church*, n. 46.

[48] Can. 251, § 2.

[49] Coetus Cardinalium peculiariter designatus, 24 mart. 1919—*AAS*, XI (1919), 251; Bouscaren, *C.L.D.*, I, 161.

[50] Can. 637, § 2, 4°.

[51] Can. 2243, §§ 1-2.

[52] Cans. 2306-2311..

[53] Can. 2287.

[54] Can. 513, § 2.

[55] Cf. can. 616, § 2.

[56] *De Curia Romana*, I, 199.

[57] Can. 1428, § 3.

cases, the religious makes his recourse not as a religious but as a pastor.[58] If the religious makes similar recourses against the decrees of the vicar or prefect apostolic,[59] the Congregation for the Propagation of the Faith should receive it. Again, if the religious belongs to an Oriental Rite, his recourse should always be addressed to the Congregaton for the Oriental Church.[60]

The Congregation for the Propagation of the Faith has competence in missionary countries, i.e. over places which have not a regular hierarchy and have not been divided into dioceses and provinces where bishops rule with ordinary episcopal jurisdiction.[61] It is possible for a country to remain under the jurisdiction of this Congregation even after a hierarchy has been established; this was true in the case of the United States, which remained subject to the Congregation for the Propagation of the Faith until 1908, even though the Province of Baltimore had been established a hundred years before. Moreover, vicariates and prefectures apostolic, although they may form a part of a province governed by the common law, remain subject to this Congregation until they become dioceses.[62]

This Congregation is likewise competent in matters relating to the foreign mission seminaries, especially as to their rules and administration.[63] It is competent to receive recourses of religious as missionaries[64] in regard to what pertains, for instance, to the administration of the sacraments and the exercise of the ministry in general.[65] Thus a religious

[58] "Idem parochus vel vicarius religiosus, licet ministerium exerceat in domo seu loco ubi maiores Superiores religiosi ordinariam sedem habent, subest immediate omnimodae iurisdictioni, visitationi et correctioni Ordinarii loci, non secus ac parochi saeculares, regulari observantia unice excepta."—Can. 631, § 1.

[59] Cans. 296, § 2, and 298.

[60] Can. 257, § 1.

[61] Can. 252, § 3.

[62] S.C. Consist., 12 nov. 1908, ad 1, XII—*AAS*, 1 (1909), 148.

[63] Can. 252, § 3.

[64] Can. 252, § 5.

[65] Ayrinhac, *Constitution of the Church*, n. 49.

missionary whose confessional office[66] or whose permission to preach[67] has been revoked, makes his recourse not to the Congregation of the Council or to the Congregation of Religious, but to the Congregation for the Propagation of the Faith.

The Sacred Congregation for the Oriental Church has jurisdiction over all matters which affect the persons or the discipline or the rite of the Oriental Churches, even if these matters are of a mixed nature, which also affect a Latin Catholic by reason either of the matter or of the person involved.[68] Its competency covers every matter relative to the Oriental Churches, except questions regarding faith and morals, regarding the Pauline Privilege, regarding dispensation from matrimonial impediments of disparity of cult or of mixed religion, regarding the scrutiny and prohibition of books, and regarding the dispensation from the Eucharistic fast for priests who wish to offer Mass, which questions are all reserved to the Holy Office.[69]

The Holy Office is the only Congregation besides the Congregation for the Oriental Church with which the Oriental Catholics must deal, since the latter possesses for the Churches of the Oriental Rites all the powers which the other Congregations enjoy for the Latin Rite. However, in the internal, even non-sacramental, forum the Sacred Penitentiary has jurisdiction over the Orientals.[70]

Consequently, an Oriental, either clerical or religious or lay, will make his recourse to the Congregation for the Oriental Church, unless the matter of his recourse is reserved to the Holy Office, as in the case of a recourse against a local ordinary's decree prohibiting the retention and reading of a certain book.[71] A Maronite priest in the United States, if he is given a precept by the Latin ordinary to whom he is subject,[72]

[66] Can. 880, § 2.

[67] Can. 1340, § 3.

[68] Can. 257, § 1.

[69] Can. 257, § 2; Cf. can. 247.

[70] S.C. pro Eccl. Or., Resp., 26 iulii 1930—*AAS*, XXII (1930), 394.

[71] Can. 1395, § 2.

[72] Cf. Leo XIII, litt. apost., *Orientalium Dignitas*, 30 nov. 1894, n. IX—*Fontes*, n. 627.

will in the event of recourse submit his plea to the Sacred Congregation for the Oriental Church.[73]

It is to these four Congregations that most of the recourses will be made, since they have jurisdiction over the majority of matters with which recourses are concerned. The other Congregations, however, receive recourses which come under their jurisdiction. For example, the Holy Office receives all recourses against an ordinary's prohibition of books.[74]

If a person is not certain to which Congregation he should address his recourse, it is advisable for him to send his petition to the Office of the Papal Secretary of State. The Secretariate will deliver the petition to the proper Congregation.

Usually, a superior intermediate to the Holy See in authority is incompetent to receive a recourse. However, the local ordinary is the competent superior to receive the recourse of a member of an association of the faithful against his dismissal from the association.[75] A religious, whose provincial superior interdicts his ascent to higher orders, may make his recourse to the moderator general of his institute.[76] By constitutions approved by the Holy See since the promulgation of the Code some superiors general are allowed to receive recourses in still other matters.[77]

The proper superior to receive a recourse against an election made by an elector who was excluded from the election is the ecclesiastical authority who has the right to confirm the election.[78]

The superior tribunal may receive recourses against a judge's declaration that he is incompetent to hear a case[79] or against his rejection of a *libellus*.[80] Finally, a recourse against

[73] S.C. pro Eccl. Or., decr. 1 mart. 1929, I, art. 10—*AAS*, XXI (1929), 153; Bouscaren, *C.L.D.*, I, 9.

[74] Can. 247, § 4.

[75] Can. 696, § 2.

[76] Can. 970.

[77] Rainer, *Suspension of Clerics*, The Catholic University of America Canon Law Studies, n. 111 (Washington, D. C.; The Catholic University of America 1937), p. 181.

[78] Can. 162, § 2.

[79] Can. 1610, § 3.

[80] Can. 1709, § 3.

a judge's failure to act on a bill of complaint is made to the local ordinary or to the higher tribunal; but to the former only if he is not the judge.[81]

The Code[82] speaks of the remedy to be used against the first decree of the ordinary removing an irremovable pastor as "recourse"; this "recourse" is made to the same ordinary who issued the decree. Consequently, this is not recourse is the proper sense of the word, since recourse is always made from a lesser superior to a higher superior. The "recourse" mentioned in canon 2153 is rather a request for a revision or a review of the acts of the case.

C. *Proper Superior for Incidental Causes.*

The Code states[83] that the law does not grant the use of an appeal to the Rota from the decrees of the ordinary, since such cases come under the exclusive competency of the Sacred Congregations. However, the Code also declares[84] that it is within the competency of the Tribunals of the Holy See to judge residential bishops and religious orders in contentious suits. From canon 1557 some argued that it was permissible to institute a contentious action against the administrative decrees, acts and dispositions of the ordinary, especially with reference to his assignment of incumbencies to benefices and offices, and to his refusal or denial of the conferal of such benefices and offices.

For example, if a priest feels that his rights have been injured when a benefice was conferred on another, why should he not be able to invoke a judicial action or suit in defense of that right? Could he not point to the principle: "Every right can be enforced by an action in court, unless the contrary is expressly stated"?[85] To justify himself in the light of canon 1601, could he not say that he is appealing or making a re-

[81] Can. 1710.

[82] Can. 2153, § 1.

[83] Can. 1601.

[84] Can. 1557, § 2.

[85] "Quodlibet ius . . . actione munitur, nisi aliud expresse cautum sit . . ."—Can. 1667.

course not against the decree of his ordinary but against the effects of that decree?

Another example is that of the priest who claims that his good reputation has been injured in consequence of an extrajudicial infliction of a censure or of a vindicative penalty. He certainly has a right to protect his good name and to demand that the ordinary repair the harm he has done. No one doubts that the priest would even have the right to demand reparation.

Finally, if by some unjust extrajudicial act of the ordinary or superior, a person has suffered a financial loss, that person has a right to demand that his loss be requited. Can that person institute a contentious judicial action in vindication of his claim?

The whole question was placed before the Code Commission. On May 22, 1923, Cardinal Gasparri (1852-1934), then the President of the Commission, replied to the question in the negative, and added the precise observation that the Sacred Congregations have exclusive competence not only over the ordinary's decrees, acts and dispositions, but also, over the impairment of rights and the damages which may have eventuated from them.[86] This reply of the President of the Code Commission was given about a month after the Rota had declared itself incompetent in such a case.[87]

The Rota case was the following. A canon had been sus-

[86] P.C.I.C., 22 maii 1923, 1°. Utrum ad normam cann. 1552-1601 institui possit actio iudicialis contra Ordinariorum decreta, actus, dispositiones, quae ad regimen seu administrationem dioecesis spectent, ex. gr. provisionem beneficiorum, officiorum, etc., aut recusationem seu denegationem collationis beneficii, officii, etc.

Et. quatenus negative,

2°: Utrum ob eiusmodi decreta, actus, dispositiones, actio iudicialis institui possit saltem ratione *refectione damnorum;* et proinde Ordinarius conveniri possit, ad normam can. 1557, § 2 et 1559, § 2 [sic.—1599, § 2], penes Tribunal Sacrae Romanae Rotae.

Resp.: *Negative ad utrumque* et ad mentem. Mens est: exclusive competere Sacris Congregationibus cognitionem tum huiusmodi decretorum, actuum, dispositionum, tum damnorum, quae quis praetendat ex iis sibi illata esse."—*AAS,* XVI (1924), 251; Bouscaren, *C.L.D.,* I, 739.

[87] S.R.R., *Diocesis X: Damnorum,* 30 apr. 1923, coram R.P.D. Francisco Parrillo—*AAS,* XV (1923), 296-302; Bouscaren, *C.L.D.,* I, 746.

pended by his ordinary for illegitimate absence from the choir on a feast day. The decree of suspension stated that there were other serious matters about which the bishop had frequently warned the canon. The canon made his recourse to the Congregation of the Council with the request that the suspension be declared invalid, and that the bishop be forced to specify and prove the grave faults alleged. The Congregation rejected the recourse. The canon again urged the recourse, especially in relation to the charge of the serious faults, since, as he said, this charge injured his good name, which had never previously been under suspicion; he further denied that he had ever received an admonition. The Congregation again rejected the recourse and added an admonition of its own.

Realizing that he had failed of success with the Congregation of the Council, the canon instituted before the Rota an action claiming damages against the ordinary because of the defamation of his character. In considering the exception taken by the ordinary against its competency, the Rota stated that it was competent over ordinaries in contentious cases when they had acted as private individuals or as subjects of rights, but that it was not competent in contentious cases when the ordinaries had acted as judges or as administrators, since in such cases competence rested respectively in the court of appeal or in the Sacred Congregations. The Rota continued:

> *"Posito hoc discrimine, iam liquido patet, Rotam incompetentem esse in iis causis videndis, quae licet Episcopum residentialem tanquam partem in iudicio habeant, originem tamen et actionem in radice repetunt a decreto administrativo vel disciplinari ipsius Episcopi. Cum enim Rota, iuxta allatum can. 1601, absolute incompetens sit in hisce causis videndis, utpote SS. Congregationibus exclusive spectantibus, consequitur eas nec in merito cognoscere, nec obiter vel incidenter in suis motivis attingere posse."*[88]

Accordingly, the Rota ruled that it was incompetent to deal

[88] *AAS*, XV (1923), 299.

with the case, and ordered the acts of the submitted question to be sent to the Sacred Congregation of the Council.

The reply of the President of the Code Commission and the decision of the Rota are in accord with the instructions Pius X gave to the Sacred Congregations, although they are broader in this instance in stating that the Rota was totally incompetent in the matter. Pius X ordered that once an administrative or disciplinary case had been instituted before a Congregation, it was not lawful to institute a judicial action in the same matter. However, the Sacred Congregation had then, as it has now, the right to refer the case to the ordinary judge in any stage of the question.[89] The Code similarly grants to the Congregations the right to refer cases to tribunals.[90]

It is therefore evident that no judicial action may be instituted on any plea that has its ultimate basis in an administrative decree, act or disposition of an ordinary. The exclusively competent superior for such incidental causes is the pertinent Sacred Congregation to which the recourse should be directed. The Congregation will decide whether and how reparation is to be made.[91]

[89] *Normae Peculiares*, Cap. III, Art. 2, 10°: "Quaestione semel instituta penes Congregationem aliquam administrationis ac disciplinae tramite, et a partibus admisso aut saltem non recusato hoc agendi modo; his iam licet eadem de causa actionem stricte iudicialem instituere.

"Eoque minus, deliberata re atque ad sententiam deducta, fas erit hic facere.

"Est nihilominus Congregationi sacrae facultas, quovis in stadio quaestionis, ad iudices ordinarios causam defere."—*AAS*, I (1909), 64.

[90] Cf. cans. 247, § 3 (Holy Office); 249, § 3 (Congregation of the Sacraments); 250, § 5 (Congregation of the Council); 251, § 2 (Congregation of Religious); 257, § 3 (Congregation for the Oriental Church).

[91] Vermeersch-Creusen, *Epitome*, III, n. 4, 1°.

CHAPTER VI

THE EFFECTS OF RECOURSE

A. *The Meaning of Suspensive and Non-Suspensive Effects*

The Code speaks of a twofold effect for both appeals and recourse., viz., suspensive *(in suspensivo)* and non-suspensive *(in devolutivo.)* The Code describes these effects thus: *"Appellatio in suspensivo exsecutionem appellatae sententiae suspendit ac propterea in suo robore manet principium: 'LITE PENDENTE NIHIL INNOVETUR'; appellatio autem in devolutivo tantum, non suspendit exsecutionem sententiae licet lis adhuc pendeat circa meritum causae."*[1]

The suspensive effect, then, denotes that the execution of a sentence or of a decree is prohibited until the entire case is reviewed, and the sentence or the decree of the lower court is confirmed, modified or reformed.[2] Thus it suspends the execution of any sentence not yet formulated and pronounced, it halts the execution of a sentence or of a decree already published or issued, and it likewise prohibits others from acting on the presumption that the sentence is valid.

The suspensive effect of an appeal or of a recourse is so comprehensive that it extends to the entire process, with the result that the cause is maintained in its previous status [namely, when a sentence or decision had not yet been rendered], and the *iudex a quo* is deprived of jurisdiction in the matter. Once an appeal has been made in a matter in which the seeking of redress entails a suspensive effect, all further proceedings of the lower court in the cause will be of no legal consequence. They simply amount to an illegal interference in procedure and an arbitrary but unavailing intervention *(attentata)*, since the Code repeats the old legal principle "While the contest is pending, let nothing be changed" (*"lite pendente, nihil innovetur"*). This suspensive effect of appeal

[1] Can. 1889, § 1.

[2] Reiffenstuel, Lib. II, tit. 28, n. 199; Pirhing, Lib. II, tit. 28, n. 228; Lega, *De Iudiciis Ecclesiasticis*, I, n. 625 and IV, n. 264; Roberti, *De Processibus*, II, n. 476; Noval, *De Processibus*, I, n. 653; Connolly, *Appeals*, p. 127.

was recognized in the Roman Law[3] and was acknowledged by Church Law.[4]

The non-suspensive effect, either of an appeal or of a recourse, denotes that the issue is brought before the superior who, while he takes cognizance of the case and judges on its admissibility and legality, leaves the previous sentence or decree operative in its effect.[5] If he judges that the appeal is legal and may be admitted, he will then study the matter in question. He will in due time confirm, correct or withdraw the sentence, decree or precept of the *iudex a quo*. However, even while the appeal or the recourse is pending, this circumstance in no way interferes with the jurisdiction of the *iudex a quo*, nor does it retard the execution of the sentence. The authority from whom the appeal is made remains unimpeded in carrying out his sentence, decree or precept in regard to his subject, except that he must do nothing to interfere with the redress that is being sought. This non-suspensive effect of an appeal is mentioned both in the Roman Law of the Emperor Justinian (527-565)[6] and in the Gregorian Decretals (1234).[7]

Every legitimate appeal and recourse operate with at least a non-suspensive effect. But in accord with the law appeals and recourses can operate also with suspensive effect.

The Code states that a judicial appeal will operate with a suspensive effect unless in particular cases the law expressly states otherwise.[8] Church Law has always conceded this generally applicable suspensive effect to appeal.[9] The suspensive

[3] "Appellatione interposita, sive recepta sive non, medio tempore nihil novari oportet".—D. (49. 7) 1.

[4] C. 12, C. II, q. 1; cc. 2, 31, C II, q. 6; c. 19, X, *de iudiciis*, II, 1; cc. 16, 34, 40, 49, X, *de appellationibus, recusationibus, et relationibus*, II, 28; cc. 4, 6, 7, *de appellationibus*, II, 15, in VI°.

[5] Reiffenstuel, Lib. II, tit. 28, n. 203; Pirhing, Lib. II, tit. 28, n. 237; Wernz-Vidal, *Ius Canonicum*, VI, n. 607; Vermeersch-Creusen, *Epitome*, III, n. 240; Roberti, *De Processibus*, II, n. 477; Blat, *Commentarium Textus Codicis Iuris Canonici* (5 vols. in 6, Romae: Collegio "Angelico", 1919-1927), IV (*De Processibus*), n. 419—hereinafter cited as De Processibus.

[6] C. (7. 62) 6.

[7] C. 55, X, *de appellationibus, recusationibus, et relationibus*, II, 28.

effect was so characteristic of judicial appeal that pre-Code authors mentioned it as a mark distinguishing it from extrajudicial appeal.[10]

B. *The Effects Specifically Determined for Particular Cases.*

In seventeen cases the Code specifically designates the effect which attaches to the making of some determined recourse. In three matters the recourse is *in suspensivo:*

1) when a recourse is made against an ordinary's action suppressing a house of a religious community of diocesan right;[11]
2) when a recourse is invoked by a religious against a decree of dismissal from the institute in which he has pronounced temporary vows;[12]
3) when a recourse is invoked against vindicative penalties which have already been inflicted.[13]

In two other cases the wording of the Code is such that a hasty reader could feel inclined to interpret it as implying that the recourse is *in suspensivo.* Dealing with a candidate who was presented as second choice to the local ordinary for incumbency in a benefice and thereupon was rejected, canon

[8] Can. 1889, § 2.

[9] C. 28, X, *de officio et potestate iudicis delegati,* I, 29; c. 19, X, *de iureiurando,* II, 24; c. 55, X, *de appellationibus, recusationibus, et relationibus,* II, 28; S.C. Ep. et Reg., decr. 16 oct. 1600—*Fontes,* n. 1586.

[10] Reiffenstuel, Lib. II, tit. 28, n. 11; Schmalzgrueber, Lib. II, tit. 28, n. 5; Ferraris, *Bibliotheca,* I, 292.

[11] Can. 498.

[12] Can. 647, § 2, 4°. The wording of this canon is unique in its explicit description of the suspensive effect. It does not read "*in suspensivo,*" but "*pendente recursu, dismissio nullum habet iuridicum effectum.*" The legislator seems to have been conscious of the many religious who could be affected in the matter of dismissal by this canon. Many of these religious naturally would be lay men and women who have no knowledge of canonical terminology. Some could be totally uneducated, and accordingly would need to have the law read and explained to them. So the legislator used the clearest and simplest language which can be understood by even the most uneducated of religious. This same condition seems to have been in the mind of the Sacred Congregation of Religious when it advised superiors to inform dismissed religious that they have the right to make recourse within ten days. Cf. S.C. de Religiosis, 20 iul. 1923, ad 3°—*AAS,* XV (1923), 457.

[13] Can. 2287.

1465, §1, states that either the patron or the presentee may have recourse to the Holy See, and then adds: *"quo pendente [recursu], suspendatur collatio usque ad finem controversiae et interim, si opus est, oeconomum ecclesiae vel beneficio vacanti Ordinarius praeficiat."* Similarly, canon 2146, §3, speaking of the recourse invoked by a removed or transferred pastor against the definitive decree of the administrative process, states: *"Pendente recursu, Ordinarius paroeciam vel beneficium quo clericus privatus sit, alii stabiliter conferre nequit."*

Actually these canons do not say that the recourse has the effect of suspending the decision or decree of the ordinary. The recourse in its primary intent is without a suspensive effect.[14] It is true, of course, that there is no canon which explicitly states that the two recourses here mentioned operate only *in devolutivo;* but the Code itself implies this when it prescribes that during the recourse the ordinary is not to confer the parish or benefice on another. This prescript would be entirely unnecessary if the recourse actually operated *in suspensivo.* As Noval says,[15] this is an occasion for the use of the principle, *"inclusio unius, exclusio alterius"*; by the specific inclusion of the one suspensive effect, the Code means to exclude all other suspensive effects.

There is, however, one suspensive effect inherent in the recourses mentioned in canons 1465, §1, and 2146, §3, viz., the conferral of the benefice is forbidden until the recourse has been settled by the Holy See.

Suarez[16] and Vermeersch-Creusen[17] hold that the decree

[14] The following authors discuss canon 2146, § 3: Suarez, *De Remotione Parochorum,* n. 23; Vermeersch-Creusen, *Epitome,* III, n. 346, 3°; Noval, *De Processibus,* II, n. 510; Connor, *The Administrative Removal of Pastors,* The Catholic University of America Canon Law Studies, n. 104 (Washington, D. C.: The Catholic University of America, 1937), p. 139; Reilly, *Residence of Pastors,* p. 65; Meier, *Penal Administrative Procedure against Negligent Pastors,* p. 198; *Regatillo, Institutiones Iuris Canonici* (2 vols., Santander, Aldus S. A., 1941-1942), II, n. 805—hereinafter cited as Institutiones.

[15] *Loc. cit.*

[16] *De Remotione Parochorum,* n. 23: "Attamen, quoad stabilem collationem paroeciae alteriusve beneficii quo clericus privatus fuerit, re-

of the ordinary is in its efficacy practically suspended. Suarez states that the recourse so affects the definitive decree that the parish does not become *de iure* vacant.

However, Connor states: "This recourse to the Holy See is *in devolutivo,* i.e. the ordinary's decree of removal is effective even while the recourse is pending. One of the effects of the recourse, however,—and this is a departure from the general rule—is to suspend the ordinary's power to confer the parish permanently on another. In that event and to that extent the recourse is *in suspensivo.*"[18] Vidal (1867-1938),[19] Noval,[20] Meier,[21] and Regatillo[22] hold the same opinion as does Connor. According to these authors the ordinary's definitive decree has its effects regardless of the recourse. The suspensive effect granted by these canons does not extend to the essence of the decision or the decree of the ordinary, but only to a mediate effect of the decree, i.e. the suspension of the ordinary's power to confer the parish or benefice.

The writer feels that this latter opinion is the correct one. It seems to agree better with the wording of the Code: "While the recourse is pending, the ordinary cannot validly confer in a permanent way on another the parish or benefice of which the cleric has been deprived."[23] If the definitive decree had been suspended, why should the Code speak of "the parish or benefice of which the cleric has been deprived"? If the definitive decree had been suspended, the cleric would

cursus est in suspensivo; nam, ipso perdurante, Ordinarius nequit tale beneficium alii stabiliter ac valide conferre; nondum enim ad normam iuris vacavit."

[17] *Epitome,* III, n. 346, 3°: "Recursum eo sensu *in devolutivo* est quod clericus beneficium liberum relinquere quam primum debet; suspenditur tamen plenus decreti effectus."

[18] *The Administrative Removal of Pastors,* p. 139. Cf. Noval, *De Processibus,* II, n. 514: ". . . suspendit dumtaxat effectum *mediatum* decreti, scilicet, Episcopi facultatem conferendi alii stabiliter beneficium . . . Clericus amotus dicitur et est vere amotus, nisi amotio sit aliunde invalida."

[19] *Ius Canonicum,* VI, n. 740.

[20] *Loc. cit.*

[21] *Penal Administrative Procedure against Negligent Pastors,* p. 203.

[22] *Institutiones,* II, n. 805.

[23] Can. 2146, § 3.

still be in possession of the parish and would not be deprived of it. The opinion, moreover, accords with the *animadversio* to the reply of the Sacred Congregation of the Council which stated: "*Licet enim recursus, in casu huius canonis* [*2146*], *vim non habeat suspendendi decretum amotionis, eo tamen pendente, Ordinarii manus a limine . . . adeo ligantur ut conferre alii non possit stabiliter . . .*"[24]

In four cases the Code indicates a non-suspensive effect—"*non in suspensivo*"—for a recourse, viz:

1) against the ordinary's statutes on precedence;[25]
2) against the solution by a vicar or prefect of apostolic disputes among missionaries (both religious and seculars) regarding the care of souls;[26]
3) against the revocation of the faculty or license to preach;[27]
4) against the condemnation of books.[28]

The negative manner of the canons in stating the effect of these recourses is tantamount to implying that the act of countermanding devolves upon the one to whom the recourse is made if the efficacy of the decree is to lose its force. The reason for the use of "*non in suspensivo*" instead of "*in devolutivo*" is not clear. Possibly the Codifiers wished to stress the fact that the decrees in these cases were not suspended in consequence of the recourse. The plain fact is that the language of the Code is not always uniform. Evidently these various canons offer but another example of this lack of uniformity.

There are five cases in which according to the express statement of the Code a recourse is attended with the consequence that the effecting of any eventual change of amendment in the previous decree or precept devolves upon the one to whom the recourse is made. The recourse is designated as being "*in devolutivo tantum*" when it is invoked:

[24] *Romana et aliarum*, 14 ian. 1924—*AAS*, XVI (1924), 164.
[25] Can. 106, 6°.
[26] Can. 298.
[27] Can. 1340, § 3.
[28] Can. 1395, § 2.

1) against an ordinary's decree whereby a removable incumbent is dismissed from his office;[29]
2) against an ordinary's decree issued during the visitation of the diocese;[30]
3) against the extrajudicial decrees of the one who conducts a canonical visitation in a religious community;[31]
4) against an ordinary's decree issued for the uniting, transferring, dividing or dismembering of ecclesiastical benefices;[32]
5) against censures inflicted in the manner of a precept.[33]

In three cases the canons designate the recourse as being *"in devolutivo"*, namely when it is invoked:

1) against the mandate of a vicar or prefect apostolic regarding the government of the missions, the care of souls, the administration of the sacraments, the direction of schools, the disposal of donations made in behalf of some particular mission, and the fulfillment of the last wills or testaments made in pious favor of such a mission;[34]
2) against the removal of a pastor who is a religious; the removal may be effected by either the local ordinary or the religious superior, and the recourse may be made by the religious or by the superior or by the ordinary;[35]
3) against an ordinary's decree which interdicts to a pastor or to the canon penitentiary the office of confessor.[36]

There seems to be no difference in meaning between a recourse *in devolutivo tantum* and one *in devolutivo*. One may unite these two classes of recourses together; to them one may also add the recourses mentioned in canons 1465, § 1, and 2146, § 3, and the four cases in which the recourse has

[29] Can. 192, § 3.
[30] Can. 345.
[31] Can. 513, § 2.
[32] Can. 1428, § 3.
[33] Can. 2243, § 1.
[34] Can. 296, § 2.
[35] Can. 454, § 5. Cf. Beste, *Introductio*, p. 286.
[36] Can. 880, § 2.

a non-suspensive effect. Thus there are fourteen specified cases for which the Code grants the option of invoking a recourse which operates without a suspensive effect.

It is interesting to note the difference regarding the effect attending on the one hand to a recourse against inflicted vindicative penalties, and on the other hand to a recourse against inflicted censures. The former operates *in suspensivo*, the latter *in devolutivo*. The basis of this difference seems to be the diversity of the purposes which these penalties serve.[37]

The purpose of a censure is the correction of the delinquent.[38] The welfare of the delinquent demands that this correction be not delayed, but rather that it be accomplished as quickly as possible. The non-suspensive effect of a recourse against the infliction of such a penalty may inconvenience an innocent party, but this will be a rare case in view of the exacting canonical requirements for the valid infliction of a censure. The delict punished by a censure must be external, grave, consummated and joined with contumacy;[39] it must be such that legal prescription has not run its course against the possible infliction of a penalty,[40] and (if the censure be of a *ferendae sententiae* character) the delinquent must have persisted in his contumacy after he had received the canonical reprimand and warning.[41]

It is difficult to see how any conscientious ordinary, having satisfied himself that the above mentioned requirements have been met, could inflict a censure on a party who is really innocent. If, moreover, the censure had been imposed invalidly, there is need not of a recourse but simply of a petition for obtaining from the competent superior a declaration of nullity regarding that censure.[42]

[37] Blat, *Commentarium Textus Codicis Iuris Canonici* (5 vols. in 6, Romae: Collegio "Angelico," 1919-1927), V (*De Delictis et Poenis*), n. 117 —hereinafter cited *De Delictis et Poenis;* De Meester, *Compendium,* III, n. 1787, footnote 3.

[38] Can. 2241, § 1.

[39] Can. 2242, § 1.

[40] Can. 2233, § 1. Cf. also cans. 1702 and 1703.

[41] Can. 2233, § 2.

[42] Cf. Coronata, *Institutiones*, IV, n. 1744.

If the party admits the commission of the delict, but feels that the censure is too grave a punishment, the recourse is still *in devolutivo*. If he makes the recourse without having sought absolution, the presumption will be that he is still contumacious, and therefore is still in need of the censure as a corrective measure.[43] Prior to the imposition of the censure he was warned to cease committing the delict; yet in spite of the warning he again sinned gravely in the matter. The presumption, therefore, will not favor him, but rather will be that the penalty was just. He must observe the penalty in both the external and the internal forum while his recourse is pending.[44]

No recourse is allowed against a *latae sententiae* censure established and enacted by law. Such a recourse would amount to a recourse against the law itself, and could only be regarded as an act in defiance of the law.[45] Such a recourse would lack all juridical basis, since the justice and the formalities of the case have been established by the law itself. In a situation of this nature one could, however, request a new hearing of the case.[46]

Vindicative penalties, on the other hand, are intended directly for the expiation of delicts.[47] They can be inflicted even if the delinquent is in no way contumacious. Their primary object is the restoration of the violated social order and

[43] Cf. in relation to judicial appeal can. 1880, 8°: "Non est locus appellationi: A sententia contra contumacem, qui a contumacia se non purgaverit."

[44] Can. 2219, § 2: "At si dubitetur utrum poena, a Superiore competente inflicta, sit iusta, necne, poena servanda est in utroque foro, excepto casu appellationis in suspensivo."

[45] Regatillo, *Institutiones*, II, n. 963; Ayrinhac-Lydon, *Penal Legislation in the New Code of Canon Law* (rev. ed., New York: Benziger Bros., 1936), n. 80—hereinafter cited Penal Legislation: Rainer, *Suspension of Clerics*, p. 176.

[46] Vermeersch-Creusen, *Epitome*, III, n. 349.

[47] Can. 2286: "Poenae vindicativae illae sunt, quae directe ad delicti expiationem tendunt ita ut earum remissio e cessatione contumaciae delinquentis non pendeat."

the discouragement of the effects of bad example.[48] No major harm is done if the application of these penalties is deferred, since their purpose may still be attained at a later time. Hence the Church's legislation allows the application of these penalties to be suspended while a recourse is pending.

The question arises: what is the effect of a recourse against a precept which threatens the infliction of a *latae sententiae* censure? This constitutes a different problem from that studied in the preceding paragraphs. In this case the penalty has not yet been inflicted; it is merely threatened. The ordinary gives a precept and annexes to it a medicinal penalty which is to be automatically incurred when the precept is violated. The effect of a recourse in such a case will, according to the Code, depend upon the matter of the precept.[49]

If it is a matter in which the law allows no recourse *in suspensivo,* the recourse will suspend neither the infliction of the censure nor the observance of the precept. For example, the ordinary forbids one of his priests to read a certain book under the threat of a censure. If the priest interposes a recourse against this mandate, he must still obey it; and if he disobeys, he is suspended, since a recourse against this particular prohibition by the ordinary is *"non . . . in suspensivo."*[50]

However, if the precept is concerned with a matter in which the law does not preclude an accompanying suspensive effect for the recourse, then a recourse against the preceptive penalty is *in suspensivo,* but the obligation to obey the precept still remains, unless the recourse is made also against the observance of the precept itself. For example, a religious in temporary vows is given a precept which, while threatening a *latae sententiae* censure, bears reference to the question of dis-

[48] Can. 2286; Lega, *Praelectiones in Textum Iuris Canonici,* Vol. I *De Delictis et Poenis* (ed. altera, Romae, 1910), n. 199: "Poenae vindicativae . . . ordinatae sunt ad effectum exemplaritatis, nimirum ut per bonum exemplum delinquentis luentis, auferatur delicti malum exemplum"; Ayrinhac-Lydon, *Penal Legislation,* n. 156: "Vindicative penalties have for their primary but not exclusive object the good of the community and the expiation of crime."

[49] Can. 2243, § 2.

[50] Can. 1395, § 2.

missal from the institute, a matter in which the Code concedes a suspensive effect to a recourse.[51] The religious may have recourse against both the command and the penalty threatened for the non-observance. When he makes a recourse against both the precept and the threatened penalty, the command ceases to bind, and the penalty is not contracted, for the suspensive effect of the recourse holds in abeyance not only the threatened penalty, but also the binding power of the issued command or precept. In similar circumstances, if there be coupled with a precept the added threat of a censure, and the law grants the invoking of a suspensive recourse against the threatened *latae sententiae* censure, then a recourse against the censure alone will indeed free the subject from the observance of the censure, but not from the observance of the precept. The additional freedom from the observance of the precept could be gained only if the invoked recourse contemplated a redress against the precept itself as well as against the threatened *latae sententiae* censure attached to the precept when it was issued.[52]

Regarding the effect of a recourse invoked against a suspension inflicted by an ordinary in consequence of his private and personal but reliable knowledge *(ex informata conscientia)*, the Code is not explicit, and authors disagree. Vidal,[53] De Meester,[54] Blat,[55] Coronata,[56] Noval,[57] Vermeersch-Creusen,[58] Augustine[59] and Woywod[60] contend that in all cases this recourse is *in devolutivo tantum*. These canonists seem to base their opinion on the pre-Code legislation. Although the Council of Trent in instituting this extrajudical penalty made no explicit mention or regulation about appeal or recourse,[61]

[51] Can. 647, § 2, 4°.
[52] Can. 2243, § 2.
[53] *Ius Canonicum*, VI, n. 805.
[54] *Compendium*, IV, n. 1685.
[55] *De Processibus*, n. 801.
[56] *Institutiones*, III, n. 1636.
[57] *De Processibus*, II, nn. 510, 511, 735.
[58] *Epitome*, III, n. 381.
[59] *Commentary*, VII, 482.
[60] *Commentary*, II, n. 2023.
[61] Sess. XIV, *de ref.*, c. 1.

the Holy See declared that recourse, and not appeal, was the means of redress against this penalty,[62] and that this recourse was not *in suspensivo*.[63]

Muñiz,[64] Suarez,[65] Aryinhac[66] and Murphy[67] hold that a distinction must be made. They note that the suspension *ex informata conscientia* may be either a censure or a vindicative penalty.[68] These authors agree that, when the suspension is a censure, the recourse against it has only a non-suspensive effect, because the recourse is governed by the rule of canon 2243, §1, which grants a non-suspensive effect only to every recourse against an inflicted censure. However, they contend that when the suspension is an inflicted vindicative penalty, the effect of the recourse is governed by the rule of canon 2287, which grants a suspensive effect to every recourse against an inflicted vindicative penalty unless the contrary is expressly stated in the law. Consequently, they hold that the recourse against the vindicative penalty of suspension *ex informata conscientia* is *in suspensivo*.[69]

The opinion of Muñiz, Suarez, Ayrinhac and Murphy seems to derive from their consideration of the norm set by canon 6, 1°: *"Leges quaelibet, sive universales sive particulares, praescriptis huius Codicis oppositae, abrogantur, nisi de particularibus legibus aliud expresse caveatur."* This norm, they maintain, places in doubt the correctness of accepting a pre-Code law as a standard, when there is a new Code law

[62] S.C.C., *Lucionen.*, 8 apr. 1848, ad 2—*Fontes*, n. 4104.

[63] Benedictus XIV, const. *Ad militantis Ecclesiae*, 30 mart. 1742, § 23—*Fontes*, n. 326; S.C. de Prop. Fide, instr., 20 oct. 1884, nn. 11, 12—*Collectanea*, n. 1628.

[64] *Procedimientos Eclesiásticos* (2. ed., 3 vols.: Barcelona, 1921), I, n. 718.

[65] *De Remotione Parochorum*, pp. 214 and 261.

[66] *Penal Legislation*, n. 37 b.

[67] *Suspension ex Informata Conscientia*, p. 116.

[68] Can. 2188, 2°.

[69] Murphy (*op. cit.*, p. 117), speaking of canon 2287, says: "Nowhere is the contrary expressly stated with regard to suspension *ex informata conscientia*, and consequently there is no doubt but that the recourse from a vindictive penalty of suspension *ex informata conscientia* is *in suspensivo*."

which exactly fits the case. These authors argue then that the former legislation which regarded all recourses from this suspension *ex informata conscientia* as being non-suspensive in their effect must be revised to accord with the prescription of canon 2287. Their arguments have considerable weight but they seem to disregard the specific norm enacted in canon 2146.

Canons 2142-2146 set the norms for all the extrajudicial processes delineated in the Third Part of the Fourth Book of the Code (canons 2147-2194). The norms are to be applied—unless there is evidence that they are not applicable—not only to the summary processes against pastors but even to the infliction of the suspension *ex informata conscientia.* There is no reason to doubt that canon 2146, §1, applies to a suspension *ex informata conscientia.* This paragraph of the canon reads: "From a definitive decree there is only one legal remedy, namely recourse to the Apostolic See." In a previous review of canon 2146 the present writer has concluded that it accords only a non-suspensive effect to a recourse against the definitive decrees of removal, transfer, etc.[70] Since the Code does not except from this norm the suspension *ex informata conscientia* which is inflicted as a vindicative penalty, one must conclude that this same norm is to be applied in the case of such a recourse. Canon 2287 does not set a general absolute norm; the norm it sets is modified by means of the clause, "*nisi aliud expresse in iure caveatur.*" Now, canon 2146 does furnish a specific norm to the contrary. Hence canon 2146 is to be regarded as exemplifying an application of the "*nisi*" clause of canon 2287. One may not regard canon 2287 as furnishing an absolute norm—for it is not such a norm,—which nullifies the application of the rule of canon 2146 to a recourse invoked against the suspension inflicted *ex informata conscientia.* If that were the correct interpretation and understanding of the norm enacted in canon 2287, then this canon would with equal force nullify the import of canon 2146 in relation to any and all of the vindicative penalties mentioned in the law as contained in canons 2147-2185.

[70] Cf. *supra*, pp. 89-92.

To bolster the conclusion which is here defended, one may point to the evident fact that there is in this matter at least a real doubt that the pre-Code law in this regard has been abolished. Canon 6, 4°, states: *"In dubio num aliquod canonum praescriptum cum veteri iure discrepet, a veteri iure non est recedendum."* Therefore, in regard to the recourse against a vindicative penalty of suspension, inflicted *ex informata conscientia,* one will look to the pre-Code law for the norm. That norm indicated that any and every such recourse operated with a merely non-suspensive effect.[71]

Regarding the effect of a recourse made by religious in perpetual vows against a decree of dismissal, there is need of making a distinction. If the religious belongs to an institute of diocesan approval, the decree of dismissal is issued by the ordinary of the place where the religious house of the professed is located;[72] the Code directs that this ordinary proceed *"ad norman can. 647."* This clearly implies that the norm of canon 647 is to be applied to the recourse of the religious in perpetual vows in an institute of diocesan approval against a decree of dismissal, and that, therefore, this recourse, if made within ten days *tempus utile,* will suspend the operative effect of the ordinary's decree.[73]

But in the case of the dismissal of women religious with solemn vows,[74] and of women religious with perpetual simple vows in an institute of pontifical approval,[75] the collected acts and documents are sent to the Holy See, and the Sacred Congregation of Religious issues the decree of dismissal. In these cases the transmission of the acts and documents becomes the practical equivalent of the making of a recourse. Against the decree of dismissal a request for a new hearing will still be allowed, but only with a non-suspensive effect, since the

[71] S.C. de Prop. Fide, instr., 20 oct. 1884, nn. 11, 12—*Collectanea,* n. 1628.

[72] Can. 652, § 1.

[73] Can. 647, § 2, 4°. Cf. Coronata, *Institutiones,* I, n. 650; Schaefer, *De Religiosis,* n. 582, a; O'Leary, *Religious Dismissed after Perpetual Profession,* p. 50; Vermeersch, "Annotationes"—*Periodica,* XII (1923), 102.

[74] Can. 652, § 2.

[75] Can. 652, § 3..

decree of the Holy See takes effect immediately upon its reception by the dismissed religious.[76]

In the case of men religious in non-exempt institutes of pontifical approval, the decree of dismissal is issued by the supreme moderator, but it must be confirmed by the Congregation of Religious.[77] Once the decree has been confirmed, any interposed request for a new hearing will have merely a non-suspensive effect.[78]

For religious who take simple perpetual vows which, because they bind only as long as the religious remains in the institute, are comparable to temporary vows, the same norms for dismissal are followed as those which apply to religious in temporary vows.[79]

Men religious in exempt clerical institutes are dismissed through a judicial process.[80] Consequently, the remedy available for such dismissed religious is not administrative recourse.

The Code does not expressly state the effect of a recourse taken against the prohibition (by an ordinary or major religious superior) of a cleric's ascent to orders.[81] However, this recourse is evidently *in devolutivo.* The dismissorial letters required for licit ordination[82] are issued by the local ordinary for secular clerics[83] and for non-exempt religious[84] and by the religious ordinary for exempt religious.[85] These letters are not to be issued until the ordinary is satified that the candidate has the requisite qualifications for higher orders.[86] If the ordinary believed that the man was so unfitted for the reception of higher orders that his ascent to

[76] Schaefer, *op. cit.*, n. 582, d; O'Leary, *op. cit.*, p. 49.

[77] Can. 650, § 2, 2°.

[78] Cf. Schaefer, *op. cit.*, n. 582, d; Coronata, *Institutiones*, I, n. 650, b; O'Leary, *op. cit.*, p. 49.

[79] P.C.I.C., 1 mar. 1921—*AAS*, XIII (1921), 177; Bouscaren, *C.L.D.*, I, 309.

[80] Cans. 654-668.

[81] Can. 970.

[82] Can. 955, § 1.

[83] Can. 958, § 1, 1°.

[84] Can. 964, 4°.

[85] Can. 964, 1°, 2°, 3°.

[86] Cans. 960, § 1; 968, § 1.

them must be prohibited, he could hardly be expected to issue the required dimimissorial letters. Therefore, we must conclude that the Code implies a merely non-suspensive effect to the recourse of canon 970.

Finally, a consideration must be given to canon 2153, §1. The text of this canon[87] does not specify whether the effect of this request for a new hearing against the first decree of removal is *in devolutivo* or *in suspensivo*. However, it is evident from the canon that the decree does not take effect until the ten days have passed; it is also evident that if a recourse is made, the decree does not have its juridic effect and force until a decision has been given in the form of a definitive decree.

C. *The Effect of Recourse in Other Cases.*

Upon a completion of a study of the effect of the recourse in specified cases, it is now proper to investigate the effect of recourse in general. Does a recourse have a suspensive or a non-suspensive effect in those cases in which its effect is not expressly mentioned by the Code? In other words, do the three specified instances of recourse that imply a suspensive effect exemplify the ordinary norm and the remaining fourteen instances the exception to it, or does the application of the rule work out vice versa?

The Code offers no general statement about the usual effect that attends an administrative recourse. There is one canon which reads: *"Recursus tamen ad Sedem Apostolicam interpositus non suspendit, excluso casu appellationis, exercitium iurisdictionis in iudice qui causam iam cognoscere coepit; quique idcirco poterit iudicium prosequi usque ad definitivam sententiam, nisi constiterit Sedem Apostolicam causam ad se advocasse."*[88] But the wording of this canon indicates that there is question of recourse, not in an administrative

[87] "Contra decretum amotionis potest parochus intra decem dies recursum interponere apud eundem Ordinarium, qui, ne invalide agat, debet, auditis duobus parochis consultoribus, novas allegationes ab eodem parocho intra decem dies ab interposito recursu producendas, simul cum rationibus primo allatis, examinare, approbare, aut reiicere."

[88] Can. 1569, § 2.

matter, but in a judicial proceeding; consequently authors speak of this canon in the sense of judicial recourse.[89]

The recourse mentioned in canon 1569, §2, to the exclusion of appeal stands for any plea to the Holy See in a matter which arises during a judicial process. Such a plea, for example, is the plea for help addressed to the Holy See by one who feels that he is being unjustly treated by a tribunal which is hearing his case. The plea can be concerned with any judicial matter other than the sentence itself. Therefore, the ruling in this canon may not be regarded as establishing a norm for extrajudicial recourse.

It must be remembered that, in the discussion that follows, the matter is considered from the legal standpoint only. The morality of the non-observance of the decree, precept, penalty, etc. does not come within the immediate scope of this work. It may be true, as moralists assert, that the presumed benign favor of the ordinary or superior or the use of *epikeia* will excuse a subject from observing a difficult law or obligation which cannot be observed without great disturbance and upset.[90] Vermeersch[91] and Rodrigo[92] make it clear that they consider that the suspension, in this case of great hardship entailed in the observance of the law, is effected not by the recourse itself, but by the presumption of the will of the superior in particular cases.

Our considerations on the effect of recourse in general will seek solely to discover whether the law concedes a suspensive effect or a non-suspensive effect in those recourses to which the Code assigns no specified effect and during which recourses the decree or precept or penalty can be observed without excessive hardship or irreparable damage. Our con-

[89] Cf. De Meester, *Compendium*, IV, n. 1514; Woywod, *Commentary*, II, n. 1561; Beste, *Introductio*, p. 764.

[90] Cf. Vermeersch, *Theologia Moralis* (3. ed., 3 vols., Romae: Pont. Universitas Gregoriana, 1933), I, n. 233; Rodrigo, *Praelectiones Theologico-Moralis Comillenses*, Vol. II (Santander: Sal Terrae, 1944), n. 244; Merkelbach, *Summa Theologiae Moralis ad Mentem D. Thomae et ad Normam Iuris Novi* (ed. altera recognita, 3 vols., Parisiis: Desclée de Brouwer, 1935-1936), n. 334, A.

[91] *Loc. cit.*

[92] *Loc. cit.*, footnote.

cern is with recourses taken against the decrees, precepts, penalties, etc., enacted by the ordinary or superior within the limits of his powers. If the ordinary or superior has exceeded his powers, his action was invalid and, consequently, there is no legal obligation to observe his mandates.

In the pre-Code law authors held that supplication operated always *in devolutivo.*[93] They could point for proof to a gloss on the Decretals of Pope Gregory IX which read: "... *appellatione interposita, nil est innovandum; sed pendente supplicatione mandatur sententia executioni, posita cautione quod omnia restituat si sententia fuerit retractata.*"[94] This gloss was based on the Roman Law of the Emperor Justinian: "*Iubemus executionem causae sine fideiussione procedere, retractationis iure servando illi.*"[95] The non-suspensive effect of supplication was to be expected, since supplication was an extraordinary remedy to be used when no other means of redress was available. It has never been the canonical practice to suspend jurisdiction merely for the reason that an extraordinary measure has been taken.

The pre-Code *recursus ad principem* was very similar to supplication. Like supplication, the *recursus ad Principem* usually had only a non-suspensive effect. Benedict XIV (1740-1758) after furnishing a lengthy list of matters in which there could be no extrajudicial appeal *in suspensivo,* stated that in these same matters either recourse or appeal *in devolutivo* was permitted.[96] The position of the words in his statement is such that one must conclude that the words "*in devolutivo*" modify not "*recursus*" but only "*appellatio.*"[97] This implies

[93] Reiffenstuel, Lib. II, tit. 28, n. 22; Schmalzgrueber, Lib. II, tit. 28, n. 3; Van Espen, *Scripta Omnia* (4 vols., Lovanii: 1753), II, 259; Bonal, *Institutiones Canonicae ad Usum Seminariorum* (4. ed., 2 vols.: Parisiis, 1898), II, 591; Theodorus a Ried-Brig, *Manuale Practicum,* n. 216.

[94] *Glossa Ordinaria* s. v. *supplicavit* in c. 4, X, *de in integrum restitutione,* I, 41.

[95] N. (119. 5).

[96] Const., *Ad militantis Ecclesiae,* 30 mart. 1742, n. 38—*Fontes,* n. 326.

[97] "Adversus Decreta Mandata et Provisiones eiusmodi, quas, vel quae ab Episcopis, aliisque Locorum Ordinariis fieri, vel capi contigerit

that he regarded *"recursus"* and *"appellatio in solo devolutivo"* as equivalent so far as their effects were concerned. In the light of this the conclusion seems warranted that he regarded recourse as always having simply a non-suspensive effect. Moreover, Lega[98] stated that pre-Code canonists often used the word *"recursus"* to describe an extrajudicial appeal that lacked a suspensive effect.

Similarly, pre-Code law allowed to extrajudicial appeal merely a non-suspensive effect in most matters.[99] Authors mentioned the non-suspensive effect as a point of difference between extrajudicial appeal and judicial appeal, which latter usually had a suspensive effect.[100]

Since modern recourse has its fundamental basis in supplication, in the *recursus ad Principem* and in extrajudicial appeal—although it now differs from them in some points—one may rightly, according to canon 6, 3°,[101] argue that since the Code gives no general norm to regulate the effect of recourse in general, and since its three juridical predecessors operated with a merely non-suspensive effect, recourse will operate with the same non-suspensive effect.

As was stated in the opening chapter, the rights of appeal and recourse are connected with the right of defense, and consequently these rights in substance derive from the natural law. The formalities, however, which attach to their exercise derive from positive human law. The natural law concept of

in Causis et negotiis praedictis, vel simplex dumtaxat, et extraiudicialis Recursus per viam supplicis libelli, ad Nos, et Successores Romanos Pontifices, vel respective, et iuxta causarum naturam, et qualitatem, appellatio ad quos de Iure, in solo devolutivo . . . recipi, et admitti possit."

[98] *De Iudiciis Ecclesiasticis*, I, n. 656.

[99] Cc. 17, 19, 46, X, *de electione et electi potestate*, I, 6; Benedictus XIV, const., *Ad militantis Ecclesiae*, 30 mart. 1742—*Fontes*, n. 326.

[100] Panormitanus, tit. *de appellationibus*, (II, 51, 10); Hostiensis, tit. *de appellationibus*, cap. 50, § 12; Reiffenstuel, Lib. II, tit. 28, n. 10; Schmalzgrueber, Lib. II, tit. 28, n. 5; Verani, Tom. II, Lib. II, tit. 28, n. 8; Ferraris, *Bibliotheca*, I, 292; Lancellotus, p. 172; Santi, I, 239; Wernz, *Ius Decretalium*, V, 528, footnote.

[101] "Canones qui ex parte tantum cum veteri iure congruunt, qua congruunt ex iure antiquo aestimandi sunt; qua discrepant ex sua ipsorum sententia diiudicandi."

appeal does not postulate a suspensive effect for every appeal and recourse. In particular cases, however, in which, if there be no suspensive effect accompanying the appeal or recourse irreparable harm will be done, the natural law of justice will demand such an effect. Thus justice demands that an appeal from a sentence entailing capital punishment should delay the execution of that sentence until the appeal has been decided. The cases in which the administrative or dominative power can inflict irreparable injuries are rare. They are such cases as the dismissal of a religious, removal of a pastor, etc. In these cases the positive law of the Code protects the individual by conceding either an entirely suspensive or a partially suspensive effect to his recourse. An appeal or recourse in cases in which no irreparable harm will be done will have a suspensive effect when that effect is conceded by positive law. Positive law does concede this suspensive effect to judicial appeal,[102] but there is no express statement in the Code granting a similar effect to recourse by way of general rule and application.[103] Therefore, it is to be concluded that recourse lacks this suspensive effect unless a specific concession is made by the law.

This conclusion gains some support from canon 204, §1, which states: "*Quod quis Superiorem adit, inferiore praetermisso, non idcirco voluntaria suspenditur inferioris potestas, sive haec ordinaria fuerit sive delegata.*" It is true that this canon is not concerned solely with recourse as a remedy against the extrajudicial acts of superiors. It is concerned with the invoking of a higher authority in any matter of a non-judicial nature, such, for example, as a matter of a dispensation from a matrimonial impediment. However, voluntary jurisdiction includes, as was seen in the second chapter, legislative, administrative and coactive powers.[104] Thus voluntary jurisdiction does embrace the matters in which a recourse becomes optional for use.

It is true that canon 204, §1, speaks of approaching a

[102] Cf. Noval, *De Processibus, II*, n. 510.

[103] Can. 1889, § 2.

[104] Coronata, *Institutiones*, I, n. 282, footnote; Wernz-Vidal, *Ius Canonicum*, II, n. 375, b.

higher superior after the lesser superior, has been passed over—"*inferiore praetermisso.*" In a recourse the lesser superior is not exactly passed over; rather a redress is sought against his acts. But it must be remembered that this canon is stating a general principle for all cases of "approaching a superior" in matters of voluntary jurisdiction, and consequently it must employ general words which are applicable to all such cases. Moreover, some authors who are regarded as good canonists,[105] treat of the remedy of recourse in connection with this canon. Consequently one may assume that canon 204 refers, at least in a general way, to the remedy of recourse.

Augustine[106] and Toso [107] consider that the effects of recourse are regulated by canon 204, §1. Toso notes, furthermore, that appeal operates *in suspensivo,* since it is of the very nature of judicial power to settle controversies. When appeal is made the judicial determination of a right or the settlement of a controversy is not yet complete and perfect; the determination or the settlement becomes strongly presumed to be complete and perfect after an appeal has been made and settled or has not been made within the stipulated time.[108] The nature of voluntary jurisdiction, however, does not encompass the settling of disputes, but rather the issuing of commands, the imposing of prohibitions or the granting of permissions in accord with established right and law. Usually there is no need to await the making and settling of a recourse or the passing of a stipulated time-limit for the recourse before the acts of voluntary jurisdiction become complete. Moreover, when a recourse is made, it is presumed—until the contrary is proved—that the superior has acted in accord with the law, and hence the efficacy of his decrees and precepts will not be suspended.

Most of the authors who discuss this question agree with Toso's conclusion, although they do not all use his arguments.

[105] E.g., Toso, *Commentaria Minora,* II, 174; Augustine, *Commentary,* II, 184.

[106] *Commentary,* II, 184.

[107] *Commentaria Minora,* II, 174.

[108] Cf. Can. 1902, 2° and 3°.

In fact, many of them give no reason for their statement that recourse usually operates with a non-suspensive effect only. Sipos,[109] Beste,[110] Vermeersch-Creusen,[111] Bouuaert-Simenon[112] and Fallon[113] offer no proof of their statements that recourse usually operates with only a non-suspensive effect.

Rainer[114] says that recourse ordinarily has a non-suspensive effect, but he bases his statement on canon 1569, § 2, which refers, as it has been noted, to judicial recourse and not to administrative recourse.

Woywod[115] and Suarez[116] refer to the Constitution *"Ad militantis Ecclesiae"* of Benedict XIV as proof of their statements that recourse usually operates *in devolutivo.* Indeed, the lengthy list of matters in which Pope Benedict allowed only recourse or appeal *"in solo devolutivo"* left very few extrajudicial matters in which an appeal *in suspensivo* could be made. Even if it is true, as some authors assert,[117] that the disciplinary dispositions of this Constitution have lost their force since the promulgation of the Code, an argument may still be drawn from Pope Benedict's use of the word "recourse" as an equivalent of the phrase "appeal *in devolutivo.*" Since this latter represents not merely a disciplinary measure, but rather an implication of the usual effects of recourse, it is not nullified simply by a later abrogation of the disciplinary measures enacted in the Constitution.

Noval[118] states that although the legislator did not enact

[109] *Enchiridion,* p. 815.

[110] *Introductio,* pp. 774, 818.

[111] *Epitome,* I, n. 320, 4°: "Simplex recursus ad Superiorem maiorem non suspendit iurisdictionem voluntariam inferioris." It must be conceded that it is not entirely clear whether the authors here refer to the remedy of recourse or to any plea addressed to a higher superior.

[112] *Manuale Juris Canonici ad Usum Seminariorum* (3. ed., 3 vols., Liége: H. Dessain, 1930-1931), I, n. 285.

[113] "Notes and Queries, Canon Law"—*The Irish Ecclesiastical Record,* Series 5, L (1937), 538.

[114] *Suspension of Clerics,* p. 175.

[115] *Commentary,* II, n. 2083.

[116] *De Remotione Parochorum,* n. 21, p. 19.

[117] E.g., Coronata, *Institutiones,* IV, n. 1744.

[118] *De Processibus,* II, n. 510: "Hoc argumentum roboratur ex eo quod, perpensis singulis canonibus tractantibus de iuris remedio quod dicitur

any express general rule on the effects of recourse in general, one may nevertheless conclude that recourse operates *in devolutivo* because the law of the Code for the sake of the common good allows so very few cases in which a recourse is to operate with suspensive effect. At a first reading of his statement one might think that Noval's argument contains a *petitio principii.* Actually, his contention is that the common good demands that episcopal decrees and precepts be obeyed. Administrative havoc could result if, in general, episcopal precepts or decrees could be retarded in their efficacy through the use of a suspensive recourse. The ordinary's authority would, as a result of this, be undermined.[119]

If it were the ordinary occurrence for a recourse to operate with a suspensive effect, it would equivalently imply that papal approval is required before an episcopal decree or precept begins unconditionally to demand obedience. Such an implication is certainly out of harmony with the Code which speaks of penalties for those who pertinaciously fail to comply with the legitimate commands and prohibitions of their proper ordinary.[120] The bishop has the right to govern his diocese in both spiritual and temporal matters;[121] cor-

recursus, apparet quod legislator, etsi non constituerit expressis omnino verbis legem generalem in qua dicatur recursum dari semper in devolutivo tantum nisi aliud in iure expresse caveatur, tamen eam legem practice induxit, eo quod contra eam legem, suapte naturam seu ratione beni [boni] publici, generalem, ut statim exponemus, paucissimas admittit exceptiones, eas videlicet relatas in cc. 647, § 2, 1465, § 1, 1709, 2153, § 1, 2243, § 2, 2287."

[119] "However, although appeal or recourse from it (episcopal authority) is admissible, it is recognized that the procedure thereto must be such as to preserve the respect due to episcopal authority and the general order of the diocesan organization. Consequently, the intrinsic efficacy and force of episcopal jurisdiction is well evidenced in the fact that the reference of matters to higher authority is generally not suspensive of the bishop's decision, so that most frequently until an appeal is taken and allowed or until the recourse which was had results in the bishop's action being overruled, his decisions stand and bind in conscience."—Ryan, *Principles of Episcopal Jurisdiction,* pp. 85-86.

[120] Can. 2331, § 1.

[121] Can. 335, § 1.

responding to this right is the juridic duty of clerics[122] and the moral obligation of the clergy and the laity to obey,[123] so long as the ordinary has not exceeded his jurisdiction. If the ordinary does command something that is beyond his powers, his precept or decree is invalid. However, if there is any doubt whether the matter be within his jurisdiction, the juridic presumption will favor the ordinary.[124]

Ryan[125] and Regatillo[126] also draw an argument from the consideration of the possible undermining of the ordinary's authority. Regatillo points out that if a recourse suspended the efficacy of a decree or a precept, the subject could, while the recourse was pending, totally frustrate the purpose of certain decrees and precepts. For example, if a cleric, who has no residential benefice or office, desires to take a short vacation, but his ordinary forbids him to do so;[127] then, if the efficacy of the ordinary's prohibition were suspended by means of a recourse, the cleric could have been away on his vacation and returned before the matter was settled by the Holy See.

It is a principle of public law that *"in societate necessaria ius sociale praevalet summae iurium sociorum."*[128] In a perfect society such as the Church the public good must be given preference over the right of an individual in the external forum. (We do not speak here of the internal forum, because the interior good of the individual can be superior to the ex-

[122] Can. 127.

[123] Hebrews, XIII, 17; I Thess., V, 12.

[124] Cf. Cappello, *Summa Iuris Canonici*, I, n. 299, 1: *"In dubio praesumptio stat semper pro Superiore, salvo iure recursus"*; Van Hove, *De Legibus Ecclesiasticis*, n. 86.

[125] *Loc. cit.*

[126] *Institutiones*, II, n. 805: *"Recursus ad superiorem altiorem generatim sunt in devolutivo tantum, non in suspensivo; et merito, nam si pendente recursu suspenderetur executio decreti cuiusvis, pessumdaretur superioris auctoritas; nam interea quivis posset contra decretum agere; et quamvis in recursu S. Sedes decretum confirmaret, saepe confirmatio esset inutilis, nam interea subditus fecit quod volebat, v.g., legit librum sibi prohibitum."* The example Regatillo gives, namely, of reading a prohibited book, is an unfortunate choice, since the Code (Can. 1395, § 2) prohibits a suspensive recourse from such a prohibition.

[127] Cf. can. 143.

[128] Ottaviani, *Institutiones*, I, n. 32.

ternal good of the Church.) Public welfare demands obedience from all the members of the society when what is commanded comes within the general orbit of the end of the necessary society. This is true even if, in some instances, the exterior rights of some individuals may be curtailed by the command. This principle is applicable to the Church Universal, and it should be applied also with due proportion to the government of dioceses. If a decree or disposition or precept harms the exterior right of an individual, the public good—and even the natural law—seems to demand that such an individual abide by the decree or disposition or precept until a competent authority has abrogated or modified it.

Noval[129] states that the cases in which the Code concedes a suspensive effect to a recourse are those in which the injury of a right or of the legitimate interests of a party are so clear that justice or equity demands that the superior's decision be suspended until the matter has been settled. They are cases in which irreparable injuries may be done to the individual, if the recourse has no suspensive effect. But in the majority of cases the injury of a right or of a person's interest is more obscure and doubtful, and also less direct and less irreparable than in these cases. For example, if the ordinary in accord with the norms of law,[130] assesses all beneficiaries of his diocese, no irreparable harm is done if the beneficiary pays the assessment even while the recourse is pending. The sum paid to the ordinary can and must be returned by him, if the Holy See says he had not the right to make the assessment. Again, no irreparable harm is done, if a person observes a censure while making a recourse against it;[131] if the person earnestly wished to be free from the obligation of observing the censure, he need only recede from his contumacy[132] and seek absolution.[133] So, Noval concludes that there is no need of suspending the efficacy of a superior's action in such cases even when the party has taken a recourse.

[129] *De Processibus*, II, n. 510.
[130] Cf. Can. 1505.
[131] Can. 2243, § 1.
[132] Can. 2242, § 3.
[133] Can. 2236, § 1.

A final and weighty argument is found in the *Animadversiones* to a *Resolutio* of the Sacred Congregation of the Council in 1924.[134] These *animadversiones* profess to give the criterion used by the Congregation of the Council in setting a ten day time-limit for the invoking of a recourse with the effect which canon 2146, §3, accords, and by the Sacred Congregation of Religious in placing the same time-limit on the use of the recourse mentioned in canon 647, §2, 4°.[135]

In the *animadversiones* it is stated that the ten day time-limit set for the making of the recourse is not a usual, but rather an exceptional demand. A time-limit is fixed for the use of recourse only when the recourse in some way binds the hands of the ordinary, e.g., by means of a suspensive effect, or by means of an effect similar to that which is stated in canon 2146. When this occurs, the recourse partakes more of the nature of an appeal than of a supplication,[136] which, as was previously seen, has a non-suspensive effect only. Therefore, from the *animadversiones* one may conclude that at least unofficially it is the view of the Sacred Congregations of the Council and of Religious that a recourse operates usually *in devolutivo*. This is strongly implied in the statement: *"Nimirum cum ordinario recursus meriti examen devolvat quin provisionem suspendat, quoties contrarium accidit, appellationis regulas sequi debet . . ."* The suspensive effect which attends a recourse is so unusual that it almost removes this juridical remedy from the category of recourse to place it under the classification of appeal. When this suspensive effect is present, the remedy no longer follows the usual norm with reference to the time interval during which the optional use of recourse is allowed; the suspensive effect is then something extraordinary. Thus is seems indicated that the ordinary effect of recourse is not that it suspends the efficacy of the

[134] S.C.C., *Romana et aliarum*, 14 ian. 1924—*AAS*, XVI (1924), 163-165.

[135] *"Hoc ipsum criterion sapienter nuper S.C. de Religiosis secuta est in disponendo circa facultatem concessam can.* 647, § 2, n. 4, *Religioso dimisso recurrendi adversus dimissionis decretum, 'quoad effectum suspensivum' . . ."*

[136] Cf. Reiffenstuel, Lib. II, tit. 28, n. 21.

ordinary's precept or decree, but that it accents the continuance of it until it be eventually reversed by the higher authority.

Roberti holds that recourse operates usually *in suspensivo.* He states: "*Effectus qui proprii sunt appellationis applicantur quoque, servatis servandis, recursibus in ordine administrativo.*"[137] Eichman[138] says that, since no general norms are given for recourse, one must apply analogously to this institute the norms for judicial appeal. Therefore, he assumes that recourse should have the same suspensive effect as judicial appeal has.

To apply the suspensive effect of appeal to recourse does not seem justified. In an article in the Apollinaris Roberti said that recourse is ruled by its own norms and not by the norms of appeal;[139] if he regards this as true in every other matter of the procedure of recourse, why should the singular exception be made in relation to the effects? Appeal and recourse are quite different institutions. An appeal is made from a judge to a higher tribunal within ten days, and is always concerned with a sentence. A recourse is usually made from an administrative superior to the administrative offices of the Holy See, with no fixed and limited interval of time, and it deals with a matter of administration. If these two institutions are so diverse in their use and application that they cannot follow the same norms in these regards, there is no legal justification—in the absence of an authoritative statement to the contrary—for saying that canon 1889, § 2,[140] must in relation to recourse be regarded as a *lex lata in similibus,* and that, therefore, according to canon 20, recourse like appeal will operate *in suspensivo.* The norm of canon 1889, § 2, presupposes the use of judicial power; it does not contemplate the cases in which there is an exclusive use of administrative power.

[137] *De Delictis et Poenis,* I, Pars. II, n. 288; cf. *op. cit.,* n. 290.

[138] *Lehrbuch des Grund des Codex Iuris Canonici Kirchenrecht* (4. ed., 2 vols., Paderborn: Ferdinand Schoeningh, 1934), II, p. 195.

[139] "De recursu ob reiectionem libelli"—*Apollinaris,* I (1928), 73-74.

[140] "*Omnis appellatio est in suspensivo, nisi aliud in iure expresse caveatur . . .*"

Some may argue from the wording of canon 2243, § 2, which states: "*Appellatio vero vel recursus a sententia iudiciali vel praecepto comminante censuras etiam latae sententiae nondum contractas, nec sententiam aut praeceptum nec censuras suspendunt, si agatur de re in qua ius non admittit appellationem vel recursum etiam cum effectu suspensivo; secus censuras suspendunt, firma tamen obligatione servandi id quod sententia aut praecepto mandatur, nisi reus appellationem vel recursum interposuerit non a sola poena, sed ab ipsa quoque sententia vel praecepto.*" They would stress the "*secus*" clause in the middle of this paragraph. They would interpret this clause as stating the general norm. They would, therefore, interpret the paragraph to mean that recourse against a precept which threatens a censure suspends the contraction of that censure unless the precept is concerned with a matter in which the law forbids a suspensive effect to the recourse.[141]

This writer, while acknowledging the merit of this argument, feels that the "*secus*" clause does not establish a general norm for recourses against precepts threatening censures. In the Code the usual procedure is to indicate first the general rule, and then the exceptions. Unless canon 2243, § 2, is a failure to follow this general procedure, one must look on the "*secus*" clause, not as a general norm, but as the exception to the general norm. The writer feels that this clause is equivalent to the "*nisi*" clauses found in other canons.

Those who would argue from the wording of canon 2243, § 2, might continue by stating that this paragraph allows recourse not only against the threatened penalty, but also against the precept itself. Since they interpret the "*secus*" clause as the general norm, they would say that this recourse against a precept usually has a suspensive effect. They would argue further that if a penalty is excessive but

[141] Cf. Coronata, *Institutiones*, IV, n. 1745: "Appellatio vel recursus a sententia iudiciali vel praecepto comminante censuras etiam latae sententiae nondum contractas, nisi exceptio probetur, ipsas censuras comminatas suspendunt, firma tamen obligatione servandi id quod sententia aut praecepto mandatur, nisi reus appellationem vel recursum interposuerit non a sola poena, sed ab ipsa quoque sententia vel praecepto."

the precept just, recourse can be had against the penalty alone; they then ask: if the precept is excessive, why should the subject have to await the threat of penalty before he can have a recourse with suspensive effect?

The writer feels that this argument must also be rejected. In the first place, if the precept is so excessive that the ordinary or superior exceeded his power in giving it, the precept is invalid and its observance is not obligatory. Secondly, canon 2243, § 2, grants a suspensive effect not to a recourse against a precept alone, but to a recourse "not from the penalty alone but even from the precept", in other words, to a recourse against both the penalty and the precept. To say that a suspensive effect is attached to a recourse against a precept alone is to go further than the words of canon 2243, § 2, allow.

Another creditable argument for those who hold that recourse usually has a suspensive effect could be drawn from the wording of those canons in which it is stated that recourse may indeed be made, "*sed in devolutivo tantum*".[142]

The use of the conjunction "*sed*" seems to imply something adversative, namely, that it is a departure from a rule which acknowledges the presence of a suspensive effect in recourse. However, the "*sed*" is referable not only to the usual effect of recourse, but also to the particular cases which are similar to those under consideration. Thus, the prescript of canon 192, § 2, regarding the recourse against the removal from office on the part of a removable incumbent differs from that of canon 2146, where the recourse of even a removable pastor is *in devolutivo,* but with the added proviso that the ordinary is not to appoint a new pastor until the recourse has been settled by the Holy See. In like manner, the recourse against an inflicted censure, as mentioned in canon 2243, § 1, differs in effect from the recourse against an inflicted vindicative penalty as mentioned in canon 2287, according to which this specific kind of recourse operates generally with a suspensive effect. Morever, the wording of canon 2243, § 2, may have been based on the Constitution *Ad militantis*

[142] Cans. 192, § 3; 2243, § 1.

Ecclesiae of Benedict XIV, which stated that no appeal with a suspensive effect against not only a sentence of excommunication *ab homine lata,* but also against a sentence of suspension or of interdict, was allowed, but that an appeal *"in solo devolutivo"* was permitted.[143]

It is worthy of note that every case now listed in the Code, except the one mentioned in canon 192, §3, in which the Code adds the word *"tantum"* after the phrase *"recursus in devolutivo,"* was given express consideration in the Constitution *Ad militantis Ecclesiae,* and is now still subject to the former ruling, namely, that in all these matters an appeal with a suspensive effect was not to be allowed, but either a recourse or an appeal *"in solo devolutivo"* was to be the legal remedy. Thus Benedict XIV treated explicitly of the episcopal visitation of the diocese,[144] of the visitation of religious communities,[145] of censures inflicted *ab homine,*[146] and of the union, division or dismemberment of parishes and benefices.[147]

On the other hand, Pope Benedict did not explicitly (although with respect to some points in these matters he did implicitly) include a consideration of the mandates of vicars and prefects apostolic regarding the government of the missions, the care of souls, the administration of the sacraments, the direction of schools, the disposal of donations made in behalf of some particular mission, and the fulfillment of last wills and testaments made in pious favor of such a mission;[148] nor did he explicitly consider either the removal of a pastor who is a religious,[149] or the interdicting of the confessional office of a pastor or of the canon penitentiary.[150] In the cases to which Pope Benedict gave no explicit consideration, the Code omits the word *"tantum"* after the phrase *"recursus in devolutivo."*

[143] Benedictus XIV, const., *Ad militantis Ecclesiae,* 30 mart. 1742, nn. 38, 39—*Fontes,* n. 326.

[144] *Ibid.,* nn. 6, 10, 19, 21; cf. can. 345.

[145] *Ibid.,* nn. 6, 10, 19, 20, 21, 24; cf. can. 513, § 2.

[146] *Ibid.,* nn. 38, 39; cf. can. 2243, § 1.

[147] *Ibid.,* nn. 11, 16, 34; cf. can. 1428, § 3.

[148] Cf. can. 396, § 2.

[149] Cf. can. 454, § 5.

[150] Cf. can. 880, § 2.

It seems, then, that the Codifiers had the wording of the Constitution *Ad militantis Ecclesiae* in mind when they formulated the canons in which the phrase *"recursus in devolutivo tantum"* occurs. Since, as was previously shown,[151] this Constitution offers a weighty argument that recourse generally operated *in devolutivo,* and since it applied the words *"in solo devolutivo"* to extrajudicial as well as judicial appeals, one must not overstress the import of the word *"tantum"* in those canons of the Code where it is used.

The writer feels that greater weight rests with the arguments of those who hold that recourse usually operates *in devolutivo.* It is his conclusion that, unless in particular cases the law contains a contrary prescription, a recourse will have only a non-suspensive effect. While respecting the arguments of those who hold the other opinion, he feels that a non-suspensive effect of a recourse is more in harmony with the pre-Code regulations on the effects of extrajudicial remedies, with the explanation of the cases in which the Code specifically designates the effect of a recourse, with the respect due to legitimate authority, and with the demands of the common good.

However, it should be noted as a final point that, although recourse has usually a non-suspensive effect, the superior or ordinary must keep in mind the ruling of canon 204, § 2: *"Attamen rei ad Superiorem delata ne se immisceat inferior, nisi ex gravi urgentique causa; et hoc in casu statim Superiorem de re moneat."* This prescription is based on the reverence which an inferior authority should have for its superior,[152] and certainly is applicable to cases of recourse.

Although canon 204, § 2, does not invalidate an act which is undertaken contrary to its rule, yet this rule does make such an act illict. If, for instance, the ordinary has divided a parish, and the pastor makes a recourse *in devolutivo* to the Holy See,[153] the ordinary should not start building a new church for the new parish until the recourse has been settled

[151] Cf. *supra* pp. 104-105.

[152] Cf. Ayrinhac, *General Legislation,* p. 362; Beste, *Introductio,* p. 219.

[153] Can. 1428, § 3.

by the Sacred Congregation. However, if a grave and urgent cause demands the erection of the new church, the ordinary may proceed, but he is bound to notify the Sacred Congregation which received the recourse that he has commenced the building, and he must also give the reasons for not waiting until the recourse was settled.

Again, if a pastor makes a recourse against the definitive decree of his removal from a parish, but does so only after the period of ten days *tempus utile* has passed, the prohibitory clause of canon 2146, § 3, does not apply.[154] In this case the ordinary is no longer legally prevented from appointing a new pastor, but he should not do so unless there is a grave and urgent cause. Attention must be paid not only to the gravity of the cause but also to its urgency. Not every grave cause is an urgent cause. Urgency implies that there is need for prompt action and that no delay can be suffered. Thus, if a parish is vacant, this situation affords a grave cause for the appointment of a new pastor; but it does not furnish at the same time an urgent cause, since the appointment of a parish administrator *(vicarius oeconomus)* can usually satisfy the need.

[154] Cf. S.C.C., *Romana et aliarum*, 14 ian. 1924: "*Tempus utile ad recursum interponendum . . . ad effectum* § 3, can. 2146 . . . "—*AAS*, XVI (1924), 165.

CONCLUSIONS

The following items are, in a summary fashion, some of the conclusions which have been reached in the course of the study and composition of this dissertation.

1. Recourse differs from both extrajudicial appeal and supplication, although it takes some characteristics from both these pre-Code remedies.[1] Its basis rests on justice and equity.[2]

2. Recourse is the only canonical remedy against the enactments of the legislative, executive and coactive powers of ordinaries, and against the actions of superiors who have dominative power only.[3]

3. Recourse is always made in the form of a letter.[4]

4. When a recourse has a suspensive effect, the superior *a quo* must be notified that the plea to higher authority has been made.[5] If the party fails to notify the ordinary or superior that he has made the recourse, he may not claim the specified suspensive effect of that recourse.[6]

5. Although there is no canonical requirement that a superior be notified that a recourse operative with a non-suspensive effect has been made against his decree, precept or penalty, reverence for legitimate authority and a desire for the speedy settlement of the recourse suggest that this notification be made.[7]

6. Usually there is no fixed determination of the time interval in which a recourse must be made.[8] However, when the recourse has a suspensive effect, the ten day time interval, as set for the making of a judicial appeal, must be observed;[9] but, even after the ten day time interval has lapsed, it is still possible to invoke a recourse which will operate without the

[1] Cf. *supra* pp. 13-14.
[2] Cf. *supra* pp. 11-12.
[3] Cf. *Supra* pp. 27-31.
[4] Cf. *supra* p. 37.
[5] Cf. *supra* pp. 39-41.
[6] Cf. *supra* p. 41.
[7] Cf. *supra* pp. 37-39.
[8] Cf. *supra* pp. 56-60.
[9] Cf. *supra* pp. 51-56.

suspensive effect that would have attached to a recourse made within the allotted period.[10]

7. When a ten day time-limit is stipulated for a recourse entailing a suspensive effect, the ten days are to be computed according to the norms for *tempus utile.*[11] A *dies feriatus,* however, will not interfere with the passing of the period of *tempus utile* for the making of a recourse.[12]

8. Generally, recourse has a merely non-suspensive effect when it is taken against a decree or precept or penalty of an ordinary or superior who has acted within the limits of his powers.[13]

[10] Cf. *supra* p. 61 and p. 71.

[11] Cf. *supra* pp. 64-66.

[12] Cf. *supra* p. 70-71.

[13] Cf. *supra* pp. 102-118.

BIBLIOGRAPHY

SOURCES

Acta Apostolicae Sedis, Commentarium Officiale, Romae, 1909—

Acta Sanctae Sedis, 41 vols., Romae, 1865-1908.

Bizzari, A., *Collectanea in Usum Secretariae Sacrae Congregationis Episcoporum et Regularium*, Romae, 1885.

Bruns, Theodorus, *Canones Apostolorum et Conciliorum Veterum Selecti*, 2 vols., Berolini, 1839.

Canones et Decreta Concilii Tridentini ex Editione Romana a. MDCCCXXXIV repetita, ed. Neapolitana, Neapoli, 1859.

Codex Iuris Canonici Pii X Pontificis Maximi iussu digestus Benedicti Papae XV auctoritate promulgatus praefatione et Indice Analytico-Alphabetico ab Emo. Card. Gasparri auctus, Romae: Typis Polyglottis Vaticanis, 1917. Reimpressio, 1934.

Codicis Iuris Canonici Fontes cura Emi. Petri Card. Gasparri editi, 9 vols., Romae (postea Civitate Vaticana), Typis Polyglottis Vaticanis, 1923-1939. (Vols. VII-IX ed. cura et studio Emi. Iustiniani Card. Serédi.)

Collectanea S. Congregationis de Propaganda Fide, 2 vols., Romae, 1907.

Corpus Iuris Canonici, Editio Lipsiensis II, (Friedberg), 2 vols., Lipsiae, 1879-1881.

Decretales D. Gregorii Papae IX suae integritati una cum glossis restitutae, Romae, 1582.

Decretum Gratiani emendatum et observationibus illustratum una cum glossis, 2 vols., Romae, 1582.

Denzinger, Heinrich, Bannwart, Clemens, et Umberg, Johannes, *Enchiridion Symbolorum, Definitionum, et Declarationum de Rebus Fidei et Morum*, 21-23 ed., Friburgi Brisgoviae: Herder & Co., 1937.

Hardouin, Jean, *Acta Conciliorum et Epistolae Decretales ac Constitutiones Summorum Pontificum*, 12 vols., Parisiis, 1714-1715.

Liber Sextus Decretalium D. Bonifacii Papae VIII, suae integritati cum Clementinis et Extravagantibus, earumque Glossis restitutis, Romae, 1582.

Mansi, J. D., *Sacrorum Conciliorum Nova et Amplissima Collectio*, 53 vols. in 60, Paris, Leipzig, Arnhem, 1901-1927.

Sacrae Rotae Romanae Decisiones Recentiores, ed. Farinaccius, Rubeus, et Compagnus, 25 vols., Venetiis et Romae, 1673-1697.

Schroeder, H., *Canons and Decrees of the Council of Trent*, St. Louis: B. Herder & Co., 1941.

Thesaurus Resolutionum Sacrae Congregationis Concilii, 167 vols., Romae, 1718-1908.

REFERENCE WORKS

Augustine, Charles, *A Commentary on the New Code of Canon Law*, 7. ed., 8 vols., St. Louis: B. Herder & Co., 1943.

Ayrinhac, H. A., *Administrative Legislation in the New Code of Canon Law*, New York: Longmans, Green & Co., 1930.

————, *General Legislation in the New Code of Canon Law*, New York: Longmans, Green & Co., 1933.

————, -Lydon, P., *Penal Legislation in the New Code of Canon Law*, revised ed., New York: Benziger Brothers, 1936.

Bakalarczyk, Richardus, *De Novitiatu*, The Catholic University of America Canon Law Studies, n. 36, Washington, D. C.: The Catholic University of America, 1927.

Bernardus Papiensis, *Summa Decretalium*, ed. E. A. Th. Laspeyres, Ratisbonae, 1860.

Beste, Udalricus, *Introductio in Codicem*, editio altera, Collegeville, Minn.: St. John's Abbey Press, 1944.

Blat, Albertus, *Commentarium Textus Codicis Iuris Canonici*, 5 vols. in 6, Romae: Collegio "Angelico", 1919-1927.

Bonal, A., *Institutiones Canonicae ad Usum Seminariorum*, 4. ed., 2 vols., Parisiis, 1898.

Bouscaren, T. Lincoln, *The Canon Law Digest*, 2 vols., Milwaukee: Bruce Publishing Co., 1934-1943.

Cappello, Felix M., *De Curia Romana*, 2 vols., Romae, 1911.

————, *Praxis Processualis*, Taurini, Marietti, 1940.

————, *Summa Iuris Canonici in usum Scholarum Concinnata*, 3 vols., Romae: apud Aedes Universitatis Gregorianae, 1928-1936.

————, *Summa Iuris Publici Ecclesiastici ad Norman Iuris Canonici et Recentiorum S. Sedis Documentorum Concinnata*, 2. ed., Romae: apud Aedes Universitatis Gregorianae, 1928.

Cavagnis, Felix, *Institutiones Iuris Publici Ecclesiastici Quas in Scholis Pontificii Seminarii Romani tradidit*, 2 vols. in 1, Romae, 1882.

Chelodi, Ioannes, *Ius De Personis, iuxta Codicem Iuris Canonici*, ed. altera, a sac. Ernesto Bertagnolli recognita et aucta, Tridenti: Libr. Edit. Tridentum, 1927.

Christ, Joseph J., *Dispensation from Vindicative Penalties*, The Catholic University of America Canon Law Studies, n. 174, Washington, D. C.: The Catholic University of America Press, 1943.

Clancy, Patrick M., *The Local Religious Superior*, The Catholic University of America Canon Law Studies, n. 175, Washington, D. C.: The Catholic University of America Press, 1943.

Cicognani, H., *Canon Law*, Authorized English Version by the Rev. Joseph M. O'Hara, Ph.D., and the Rev. Francis Brennan, D.D., J.U.D., revised edition, Philadelphia: The Dolphin Press, 1935.

Cocchi, Guidus, *Commentarium in Codicem Iuris Canonici ad Usum Scholarum*, 8 vols., Taurini: Marietti, 1920-1930.

Connolly, Thomas A., *Appeals*, The Catholic University of America Canon Law Studies, n. 79, Washington, D. C.: The Catholic University of America, 1932.

Coronata, Mattheus Conte a, *Institutiones Iuris Canonici*, 5 vols., Taurini: Marietti, 1928-1936.

———, *Ius Publicum Ecclesiasticum*, 2 ed., Taurini: Marietti, 1934.

De Angelis, Phillipus, *Praelectiones Iuris Canonici ad methodum Decretalium Gregorii IX exactae*, ed. a Nazareno Gentilini, 5 vols. in 9, Romae, 1877-1891.

De Camillis, Iosephus, *Institutiones Iuris Canonici*, 3 vols., Parisiis, 1868.

De Meester, A, *Juris Canonici et Juris Canonico-Civilis Compendium*, ed. nova, 3 vols. in 4, Brugis, 1921-1928.

Doheny, William J., *Canonical Procedure in Matrimonial Cases*, Milwaukee, Bruce Publishing Co., 1938.

Droste, Francis—Messmer, Sebastian, *Canonical Procedure in Disciplinary and Criminal Cases of Clerics*, New York, 1887.

Dubé, Arthur J., *The General Principles for the Reckoning of Time in Canon Law*, The Catholic University of America Canon Law Studies, n. 144, Washington, D. C.: The Catholic University of America Press, 1941.

Durandus, (Durantis), Gulielmus, *Speculum Iuris*, Venetiis, 1577.

Eichman, Eduard, *Lehrbuch des Grund des Codex Iuris Canonici Kirchenrecht*, 4. ed., 2 vols., Paderborn: Ferdinand Schoeningh, 1934.

Esswein, Anthony A., *The Extrajudicial Coercive Powers of Ecclesiastical Superiors*, The Catholic University of America Canon Law Studies, n. 127, Washington, D. C.: The Catholic University of America Press, 1941.

Fagnanus, P., *Commentaria in Quinque Libros Decretalium*, 5 vols. in 3, Coloniae Allobrogum, 1759.

Fanfani, Ludovicus I., *De Iure Religiosorum ad Norman Codicis Iuris Canonici*, ed. altera, Taurini: Marietti, 1925.

Fermosinus, Nicholaus, *Opera Omnia, Canonica, Civilia, et Criminalia*, 14 vols., Coloniae Allobrogum, 1741.

Ferraris, Lucius, *Prompta Bibliotheca Canonica, Iuridica, Moralis, Theologica necnon Ascetica, Polemica, Rubristica*, 9 vols., Romae, 1885-1899.

Funk, F. X., *A Manual of Church History*, trans. from 5. German ed., 2 vols., St. Louis: Herder & Co., 1910.

Grandeclaude, E., *Ius Canonicum iuxta Ordinem Decretalium*, 3 vols., Parisiis, 1882-1883.

Hostiensis, Cardinalis (Henricus de Segusio), *Commentaria in Quinque Decretalium Libros*, 5 vols. in 3, Venetiis, 1581.

Jaeger, Leo, *The Administration of Vacant and Quasi-Vacant Episcopal Sees in the United States*, The Catholic University of America Canon Law Studies, n. 81, Washington, D. C.: The Catholic University of America, 1932.

Jaffé, P., *Regesta Pontificum Romanorum ab condita Ecclesia ad annum post Christum natum* 1198, editionem secundam correctam et auctam auspiciis Gulielmi Wattenbach curaverunt S. Löwenfeld, F. Kaltenbrunner, P. Ewald, 2 vols. in 1, Lipsiae, 1885-1888.

Kealy, John J., *The Introductory Libellus in Church Court Procedure*, The Catholic University of America Canon Law Studies, n. 108, Washington, D. C.: The Catholic University of America, 1937.

Lega, Michael, *Praelectiones in Textum Iuris Canonici De Iudiciis Ecclesiasticis in Scholis Pont. Sem. Rom. Habitae*, 4 vols., Romae, 1896-1901. Vols. III-IV revised in 1 vol. *De Delictis et Poenis*, Romae, 1910.

Meier, Carl A., *Penal Administrative Procedure against Negligent Pastors*, The Catholic University of America Canon Law Studies, n. 140, Washington, D. C.: The Catholic University of America Press, 1941.

Merkelbach, Benedictus H., *Summa Theologiae Moralis ad Mentem D. Thomae et ad Norman Iuris Novi*, ed. altera recognita, 3 vols., Parisiis: Desclée de Brouwer, 1935-1936.

Michiels, G., *Normae Generales Iuris Canonici*, 2 vols., Lublin: Universitas Catholica, 1929.

Migne, Jacques Paul, *Patrologiae Cursus Completus, Series Graeca*, 161 vols., Parisiis, 1856-1866.

———, *Patrologiae Cursus Completus, Series Latina*, 221 vols., Parisiis, 1844-1864.

Monin, Arthur, *De Curia Romana*, Lovanii, 1912.

Muñiz, T., Procedimientos Eclesiásticos, 2 ed., 3 vols., Barcelona, 1921.

Murphy, Edwin J., *Suspension ex Informata Conscientia*, The Catholic University of America Canon Law Studies, n. 76, Washington, D. C.: The Catholic University of America, 1932.

Noval, Josephus, *Commentarium Codicis Iuris Canonici*, Lib. IV, *De Processibus*, 2 vols., Romae: Marietti, 1920-1932.

Oesterle, Gerardus, *Praelectiones Iuris Canonici*, Vol. I, Romae: ex Officina Typographica 'Cuore di Maria', 1931.

Ojetti, B., *Synopsis Rerum Moralium et Iuris Pontificii*, 3. ed., 4 vols., Romae, 1909-1914.

O'Leary, Charles G., *Religious Dismissed after Perpetual Profession*, The Catholic University of America Canon Law Studies, n. 184, Washington, D. C.: The Catholic University of America Press, 1943.

O'Neill, Francis J., *The Dismissal of Religious in Temporary Vows*, The Catholic University of America Canon Law Studies, n. 166, Washington, D. C.: The Catholic University of America Press, 1942.

Ottaviani, Alaphridus, *Institutiones Iuris Publici Ecclesiastici*, 2. ed., 2 vols., Civitate Vaticana: Typis Polyglottis Vaticanis, 1935-1936.

Panormitanus, Abbas (Nicolaus de Tudeschis), *Commentaria in Quinque Libros Decretalium*, 5 vols. in 8, Venetiis, 1588.

Papi, Hector, *The Government of Religious Communities*, New York, 1919.

Pejška, Iosephus, *Ius Canonicum Religiosorum*, 3. ed., Friburgi Brisgoviae: B. Herder Co., 1927.

Pirhing, Ernricus, *Ius Canonicum*, ed. noviss., 5 vols. in 4, Dilingae, 1722.

Pistocchi, M., *De Re Beneficiali iuxta Canones*, Taurini: Marietti, 1928.

Prümmer, Dominicus, *Manuale Iuris Canonici*, 3. ed., Friburgi Brisgoviae, 1922.

Rainer, Eligius, *Suspension of Clerics*, The Catholic University of America Canon Law Studies, n. 111, Washington, D. C.: The Catholic University of America, 1937.

Regatillo, Eduardus F., *Institutiones Iuris Canonici*, 2 vols., Santander, Aldus S.A., 1941-1942.

Reiffenstuel, A., *Ius Canonicum Universum*, 5 vols. in 7, Parisiis, 1864-1870.

Reilly, Peter, *Residence of Pastors*, The Catholic University of America Canon Law Studies, n. 97, Washington, D. C.: The Catholic University of America, 1935.

Roberti, Franciscus, *De Processibus*, 2 vols. in 1, Romae: apud Aedes Facultatis Iuridicae S. Apollinaris, 1926.

———, *De Delictis et Poenis*, Vol. I, Partes I & II, Romae: Librariam Pontificii Instituti Utriusque Iuris, 1938.

Rodrigo, Lucius, *Praelectiones Theologico-Moralis Comillenses*, Vol. II, Santander: Sal Terrae, 1944.

Romani, Sylvius, *Summa Iuris Canonici Lineamenta*, Romae: ex Typographia Missionaria Dominicana, 1939.

Rufinus, *Summa Decretorum*, ed. H. Singer, Paderborn, 1902.

Ryan, Gerald A., *Principles of Episcopal Jurisdiction*, The Catholic University of America Canon Law Studies, n. 120, Washington, D. C.: The Catholic University of America Press, 1939.

Santi, Franciscus, *Praelectiones Juris Canonici juxta Ordinem Decretalium Gregorii IX*, 2 vols., Ratisbonae, 1886.

Schaefer, Timotheus, *De Religiosis ad norman Codicis Iuris Canonici*, 3. ed., Romae: S.A.L.E.R., 1940.

Schmalzgrueber, Franc., *Ius Ecclesiasticum Universum*, 5 vols. in 12, Romae, 1843-1845.

Sipos, Stephanus, *Enchiridion Iuris Canonici*, 2. ed., Pécs, "Haladás R.T.", 1931.

Suarez, Emmanuel, *De Remotione Parochorum Aliisque Processibus Tertiae Partis Lib. IV. C.I.C.*, Romae, Pontificium Internationale Institutum Angelicum de Urbe, 1931.

Theodorus a Ried-Brig, *Manuale Practicum Juris Disciplinaris et Criminalis Regularium ad Usum F. Min. Cap.*, Romae, 1902.

Toso, Albertus, *Ad Codicem Iuris Canonici Commentaria Minora*, Vols. I-II, Taurini: Marietti, 1921-1922.

Van Espen, Z. Bernardus, *Scripta Omnia*, 4 vols., Lovanii, 1753.

Van Hove, A., *Commentarium Lovaniense in Codicem Iuris Canonici*, Vol. II, *De Legibus Ecclesiasticis*, Mechliniae: H. Dessain, 1930; Vol. III, *De Temporis Supputatione*, Mechliniae: H. Dessain, 1933; Vol. IV, *De Rescriptis*, Mechliniae: H. Dessain, 1936.

Verani, Cajetanus Felix, *Iuris Canonici Universi Commentarius Paratitlaris*, 5 vols., Monachii, 1703-1708.

Vermeersch, A., *Theologiae Moralis Principia—Responsa—Consilia*, 3. ed., 4 vols., Romae: Pont. Universitas Gregoriana, 1933-1937.

————, -Creusen, J., *Epitome Iuris Canonici*, 3 vols., Mechliniae: H. Dessain, 1934-1937: Vol. I, 6. ed., 1937; Vol. II, 5. ed., 1934; Vol. III, 6. ed., 1936.

Wernz, F. X., *Ius Decretalium*, 2. ed., 6 vols., Romae et Prati, 1898-1905.

————, -Vidal, P., *Ius Canonicum*, 7 vols. in 8, Romae: apud Aedes Universitatis Gregorianae, 1923-1938.

Woywod, Stanislaus, *A Practical Commentary on the Code of Canon Law*, 5. ed. revised, 2 vols., New York: Joseph F. Wagner, 1939.

ARTICLES

Anonymous, "Del termini di ricorso alla S. Sede nel processo di amozione dalla parochia"—*Il Monitore Ecclesiastico*, XXXVI (1924), 139-144.

Couly, A., "Le Recours Administratif"—*Le Canoniste*, XLVI (1924), 455-458.

Fallon, M. J., "Notes and Queries—Canon Law"—*The Irish Ecclesiastical Record*, 5. Series, L (1937), 537-539.

Hofmann, K., "De Iuris Remediis contra leges latas"—*Apollinaris*, VII (1934), 361.

————, "Die Rechtsmittel gegen Gusetzgebung in Kanonischen Recht" —*Acta Congressus Iuridici Internationalis* (5 vols., Romae: apud Custodiam Librariam Pont. Instituti Utriusque Iuris, 1935-1937), IV, 51-60.

Maroto, P., "Annotationes"—*Commentarium pro Religiosis*, IV (1923), 355-358.

Roberti, F., "De recursu ob reiectionem libelli"—*Apollinaris*, I (1928), 73-74.

Vermeersch, A., "Annotationes"—*Periodica*, XII (1923), 101-104.

PERIODICALS

Apollinaris, Romae, 1928—

Le Canoniste Contemporaine, Parisiis, 1878-1924; ab anno 1924-1926, *Le Canoniste*.

Commentarium Pro Religiosis, Romae, 1920—; ab anno 1935, *Commentarium pro Religiosis et Missionariis*.

Periodica de Religiosis et Missionariis, Brugis, 1905-1919; *Periodica de Re Canonica et Morali utili praesertim Religiosis et Missionariis*, 1920-1927; *Periodica de Re Canonica, Morali, Liturgica*, 1927—.

The Irish Ecclesiastical Record, Dublin, 1864—.

ALPHABETICAL INDEX

BIOGRAPHICAL NOTE

Justin D. McClunn was born in Brooklyn, N. Y., on April 13, 1916. After completing his elementary studies at St. Ephrem's Parochial School, Brooklyn, he attended Brooklyn Preparatory College and the Catholic University of America in Washington, D. C. In 1936 he entered St. Mary's Seminary, Baltimore, Md., where he completed his studies in philosophy. In 1937 he was assigned to the Sulpician Seminary in Washington, D. C., to study theology at the Catholic University of America. He was ordained to the priesthood on May 15, 1941, and shortly thereafter received the Degree of Licentiate in Sacred Theology. For two years he was assistant chancellor of the Diocese of Richmond, notary of the Diocesan Court and assistant pastor of St. Peter's Church in Richmond, Va. In June, 1943, he was appointed assistant pastor of St. Agnes' Church, Arlington, Va. In September of that year he was enrolled in the School of Canon Law at the Catholic University of America, where he received the Baccalaureate Degree in Canon Law in May, 1944, and the Licentiate Degree in May, 1945.

CANON LAW STUDIES

1. FRERIKS, REV. CELESTINE A. C.PP.S., J.C.D., Religious Congregations in Their External Relations, 121 pp., 1916.
2. GALLIHER, REV. DANIEL M., O.P., J.C.D., Canonical Elections, 117 pp., 1917.
3. BORKOWSKI, REV. AURELIUS L., O.F.M., J.C.D., De Confraternitatibus Ecclesiasticis, 136 pp., 1918.
4. CASTILLO, REV. CAYO, J.C.D., Disertacion Historico-Canonica sobre la Potestad del Cabildo en Sede Vacante o Impedida del Vicario Capitular, 99 pp., 1919 (1918).
5. KUBELBECK, REV. WILLIAM J., S.T.B., J.C.D., The Sacred Penitentiaria and Its Relation to Faculties of Ordinaries and Priests, 129 pp., 1918.
6. PETROVITS, REV. JOSEPH, J. C., S.T.D., J.C.D., The New Church Law on Matrimony, X-461 pp., 1919.
7. HICKEY, REV. JOHN J., S.T.B., J.C.D., Irregularities and Simple Impediments in the New Code of Canon Law, 100 pp., 1920.
8. KLEKOTKA, REV. PETER J., S.T.B., J.C.D., Diocesan Consultors, 179 pp., 1920.
9. WANENMACHER, REV. FRANCIS, J.C.D., The Evidence in Ecclesiastical Procedure Affecting the Marriage Bond, 1920 (Printed 1935).
10. GOLDEN, REV. HENRY FRANCIS, J.C.D., Parochial Benefices in the New Code, IV-119 pp., 1921 (Printed 1925).
11. KOUDELKA, REV. CHARLES J., J.C.D., Pastors, Their Rights and Duties According to the New Code of Canon Law, 211 pp., 1921.
12. MELO, REV. ANTONIUS, O.F.M., J.C.D., De Exemptione Regularium, X-188 pp., 1921.
13. SCHAAF, REV. VALENTINE THEODORE, O.F.M., S.T.B., J.C.D., The Cloister, X-180 pp., 1921.
14. BURKE, REV. THOMAS JOSEPH, S.T.D., J.C.D., Competence in Ecclesiastical Tribunals, IV-117 pp., 1922.
15. LEECH, REV. GEORGE LEO, J.C.D., A Comparative Study of the Constitution "Apostolicae Sedis" and the "Codex Juris Canonici," 179 pp., 1922.
16. MOTRY, REV. HUBERT LOUIS, S.T.D., J.C.D., Diocesan Faculties According to the Code of Canon Law, II-167 pp., 1922.
17. MURPHY, REV. GEORGE LAWRENCE, J.C.D., Delinquencies and Penalties in the Administration and the Reception of the Sacraments, IV-121 pp., 1923.
18. O'REILLY, REV. JOHN ANTHONY, S.T.B., J.C.D., Ecclesiastical Sepulture in the New Code of Canon Law, II-129 pp., 1923.
19. MICHALICKA, REV. WENCESLAS CYRIL, O.S.B., J.C.D., Judicial Procedure in Dismissal of Clerical Exempt Religious, 107 pp., 1923.

*Below n. 100 only the following numbers are still available: Nos. 25, 57 and 75. Beginning with n. 100 only the following numbers are unavailable: Nos. 100-111 inclusive, 113 and 115-117 inclusive.

20. DARGIN, REV. EDWARD VINCENT, S.T.B., J.C.D., Reserved Cases According to the Code of Canon Law, IV-103 pp., 1924.
21. GODFREY, REV. JOHN A., S.T.B., J.C.D., The Right of Patronage According to the Code of Canon Law, 153 pp., 1924.
22. HAGEDORN, REV. FRANCIS EDWARD, J.C.D., General Legislation on Indulgences, II-154 pp., 1924.
23. KING, REV. JAMES IGNATIUS, J.C.D., The Administration of the Sacraments to Dying Non-Catholics, V-141 pp., 1924.
24. WINSLOW, REV. FRANCIS JOSEPH, O.F.M., J.C.D., Vicars and Prefects Apostolic, IV-149 pp., 1924.
25. CORREA, REV. JOSE SERVELION, S.T.L., J.C.D., La Potestad Legislativa de la Iglesia Catolica, IV-127 pp., 1925.
26. DUGAN, REV. HENRY FRANCIS, A.M., J.C.D., The Judiciary Department of the Diocesan Curia, 87 pp., 1925.
27. KELLER, REV. CHARLES FREDERICK, S.T.B., J.C.D., Mass Stipends, 167 pp., 1925.
28. PASCHANG, REV. JOHN LINUS, J.C.D., The Sacramentals According to the Code of Canon Law, 129 pp., 1925.
29. PIONTEK, REV. CYRILLUS, O.F.M., S.T.B., J.C.D., De Indulto Exclaustrationis necnon Saecularizationis, XIII-289 pp., 1945.
30. KEARNEY, REV. RICHARD JOSEPH, S.T.B., J.C.D., Sponsors at Baptism According to the Code of Canon Law, IV-127 pp., 1925.
31. BARTLETT, REV. CHESTER JOSEPH, A.M., LL.B., J.C.D., The Tenure of Parochial Property in the United States of America, V-108 pp., 1926.
32. KILKER, REV. ADRIAN JEROME, J.C.D., Extreme Unction, V-425 pp., 1926.
33. MCCORMICK, REV. ROBERT EMMETT, J.C.D., Confessors of Religious, VIII-266 pp., 1926.
34. MILLER, REV. NEWTON THOMAS, J.C.D., Founded Masses According to the Code of Canon Law, VII-93 pp., 1926.
35. ROELKER, REV. EDWARD G., S.T.D., J.C.D., Principles of Privilege According to the Code of Canon Law, XI-166 pp., 1926.
36. BAKALARCZYK, REV. RICHARDUS, M.I.C., J.U.D., De Novitiatu, VIII-208 pp., 1927.
37. PIZZUTI, REV. LAWRENCE, O.F.M., J.U.L., De Parochis Religiosis, 1927. (Not Printed).
38. BLILEY, REV. NICHOLAS MARTIN, O.S.B., J.C.D., Altars According to the Code of Canon Law, XIX-132 pp., 1927.
39. BROWN, MR. BRENDAN FRANCIS, A.B., LL.M., J.U.D., The Canonical Juristic Personality with Special Reference to its Status in the United States of America, V-212 pp., 1927.
40. CAVANAUGH, REV. WILLIAM THOMAS, C.P., J.U.D., The Reservation of the Blessed Sacrament, VIII-101 pp., 1927.
41. DOHENY, REV. WILLIAM J., C.S.C., A.B., J.U.D., Church Property: Modes of Acquisition, X-118 pp., 1927.

42. FELDHAUS, REV. ALOYSIUS H., C.PP. S., J.C.D., Oratories, IX-141 pp., 1927.
43. KELLY, REV. JAMES PATRICK, A.B., J.C.D., The Jurisdiction of the Simple Confessor, X-208 pp., 1927.
44. NEUBERGER, REV. NICHOLAS J., J.C.D., Canon 6 or the Relation of the Codex Juris Canonici to the Preceding Legislation, V-95 pp., 1927.
45. O'KEEFE, REV. GERALD MICHAEL, J.C.D., Matrimonial Dispensations, Powers of Bishops, Priests, and Confessors, VIII-232 pp., 1927.
46. QUIGLEY, REV. JOSEPH A. M., A.B., J.C.D., Condemned Societies, 139 pp., 1927.
47. ZAPLOTNIK, REV. JOHANNES LEO, J.C.D., De Vicariis Foraneis, X-142 pp., 1927.
48. DUSKIE, REV. JOHN ALOYSIUS, A.B., J.C.D., The Canonical Status of the Orientals in the United States, VIII-196 pp., 1928.
49. HYLAND, REV. FRANCIS EDWARD, J.C.D., Excommunication, Its Nature, Historical Development and Effects, VIII-181 pp., 1928.
50. REINMANN, REV. GERALD JOSEPH, O.M.C., J.C.D., The Third Order Secular of Saint Francis, 201 pp., 1928.
51. SCHENK, REV. FRANCIS J., J.C.D., The Matrimonial Impediments of Mixed Religion and Disparity of Cult, XVI-318 pp., 1929.
52. COADY, REV. JOHN JOSEPH, S.T.D., J.U.D., A.M., The Appointment of Pastors, VIII-150 pp., 1929.
53. KAY, REV. THOMAS HENRY, J.C.D., Competence in Matrimonial Procedure, VIII-164 pp., 1929.
54. TURNER, REV. SIDNEY JOSEPH, C.P., J.U.D., The Vow of Poverty, XLIX-217 pp., 1929.
55. KEARNEY, REV. RAYMOND A., A.B., S.T.D., J.C.D., The Principles of Delegation, VII-149 pp., 1929.
56. CONRAN, REV. EDWARD JAMES, A.B., J.C.D., The Interdict, V-163 pp., 1930.
57. O'NEILL, REV. WILLIAM H., J.C.D., Papal Rescripts of Favor, VII-218 pp., 1930.
58. BASTNAGEL, REV. CLEMENT VINCENT, J.U.D., The Appointment of Parochial Adjutants and Assistants, XV-257 pp., 1930.
59. FERRY, REV. WILLIAM A., A.B., J.C.D., Stole Fees, V-136 pp., 1930.
60. COSTELLO, REV. JOHN MICHAEL, A.B., J.C.D., Domicile and Quasi-Domicile, VII-201 pp., 1930.
61. KREMER, REV. MICHAEL NICHOLAS, A.B., S.T.B., J.C.D., Church Support in the United States, VI-136 pp., 1930.
62. ANGULO, REV. LUIS, C.M., J.C.D., Legislation de la Iglesia sôbre la intencion en la application de la Santa Misa, VII-104 pp., 1931.
63. FREY, REV. WOLFGANG NORBERT, O.S.B., A.B., J.C.D., The Act of Religious Profession, VIII-174 pp., 1931.
64. ROBERTS, REV. JAMES BRENDAN, A.B., J.C.D., The Banns of Marriage, XIV-140 pp., 1931.

65. RYDER, REV. RAYMOND ALOYSIUS, A.B., J.C.D., Simony, IX-151 pp., 1931.
66. CAMPAGNA, REV. ANGELO, PH.D., J.U.D., Il Vicario Generale del Vescovo, VII-205 pp., 1931.
67. COX, REV. JOSEPH GODFREY, A.B., J.C.D., The Administration of Seminaries, VI-124 pp., 1931.
68. GREGORY, REV. DONALD J., J.U.D., The Pauline Privilege, XV-165 pp., 1931.
69. DONOHUE, REV. JOHN F., J.C.D., The Impediment of Crime. VII-110 pp., 1931.
70. DOOLEY, REV. EUGENE A., O.M.I., J.C.D., Church Law on Sacred Relics, IX-143 pp., 1931.
71. ORTH, REV. CLEMENT RAYMOND, O.M.C., J.C.D., The Approbation of Religious Institutes, 171 pp., 1931.
72. PERNICONE, REV. JOSEPH M., A.B., J.C.D., The Ecclesiastical Prohibition of Books, XII-267 pp., 1932.
73. CLINTON, REV. CONNELL, A.B., J.C.D., The Paschal Precept, IX-108 pp., 1932.
74. DONNELLY, REV. FRANCIS B., A.M., S.T.L., J.C.D., The Diocesan Synod, VIII-125 pp., 1932.
75. TORRENTE, REV. CAMILO, C.M.F., Las Procesiones Sagradas, V-145 pp., 1932.
76. MURPHY, REV. EDWIN J., C.PP.S., J.C.D., Suspension Ex Informata Conscientia, XI-122 pp., 1932.
77. MACKENZIE, REV. ERIC F., A.M., S.T.L., J.C.D., The Delict of Heresy in its Commission, Penalization, Absolution, VII-124 pp., 1932.
78. LYONS, REV. AVITUS, E., S.T.B., J.C.D., The Collegiate Tribunal of First Instance, XI-147 pp., 1932.
79. CONNOLLY, REV. THOMAS A., J.C.D., Appeals, XI-195 pp., 1932.
80. SANGMEISTER, REV. JOSEPH V., A.B., J.C.D., Force and Fear as Precluding Matrimonial Consent, V-211 pp., 1932.
81. JAEGER, REV. LEO A., A.B., J.C.D., The Administration of Vacant and Quasi-Vacant Episcopal Sees in the United States, IX-229 pp., 1932.
82. RIMLINGER, REV. HERBERT T., J.C.D., Error Invalidating Matrimonial Consent, VII-79 pp., 1932.
83. BARRETT, REV. JOHN D. M., S.S., J.C.D., A Comparative Study of the Third Plenary Council of Baltimore and the Code, IX-221 pp., 1932.
84. CARBERRY, REV. JOHN J., PH.D., S.T.D., J.C.D., The Juridical Form of Marriage, X-177 pp., 1934.
85. DOLAN, REV. JOHN L., A.B., J.C.D., The Defensor Vinculi, XII-157 pp., 1934.
86. HANNAN, REV. JEROME D., A.M., S.T.D., LL.B., J.C.D., The Canon Law of Wills, IX-517 pp., 1934.

87. LEMIEUX, REV. DELISE A., A.M., J.C.D., The Sentence in Ecclesiastical Procedure, IX-131 pp., 1934.
88. O'ROURKE, REV. JAMES J., A.B., J.C.D., Parish Registers, VII-109 pp., 1934.
89. TIMLIN, REV. BARTHOLOMEW, O.F.M., A.M., J.C.D., Conditional Matrimonial Consent, X-381 pp., 1934.
90. WAHL, REV. FRANCIS X., A.B., J.C.D., The Matrimonial Impediments of Consanguinity and Affinity, VI-125 pp., 1934.
91. WHITE, REV. ROBERT J., A.B., LL.B., S.T.B., J.C.D., Canonical Ante-Nuptial Promises and the Civil Law, VI-152 pp., 1934.
92. HERRERA, REV. ANTONIO PARRA, O.C.D., J.C.D., Legislacion Ecclesiastica sobra el Ayuno y la Abstinencia, XI-191 pp., 1935.
93. KENNEDY, REV. EDWIN J., J.C.D., The Special Matrimonial Process in Cases of Evident Nullity, X-165 pp., 1935.
94. MANNING, REV. JOHN J., A.B., J.C.D., Presumption of Law in Matrimonial Procedure, XI-111 pp., 1935.
95. MOEDER, REV. JOHN M., J.C.D., The Proper Bishop for Ordination and Dimissorial Letters, VII-135 pp., 1935.
96. O'MARA, REV. WILLIAM A., A.B., JJ.C.D., Canonical Causes for Matrimonial Dispensations, IX-155 pp., 1935.
97. REILLY, REV. PETER, J.C.D., Residence of Pastors, IX-81 pp., 1935.
98. SMITH, REV. MARINER T., O.P., S.T.Lr., J.C.D., The Penal Law for Religious, VII-169 pp., 1935.
99. WHALEN, REV. DONALD W., A.M., J.C.D., The Value of Testimonial Evidence in Matrimonial Procedure, XIII-297 pp., 1935.
100. CLEARY, REV. JOSEPH F., J.C.D., Canonical Limitations on the Alienation of Church Property, VIII-141 pp., 1936.
101. GLYNN, REV. JOHN C., J.C.D., The Promoter of Justice, XX-337 pp., 1936.
102. BRENNAN, REV. JAMES H., S.S., M.A., S.T.B., J.C.D., The Simple Convalidation of Marriage, VI-135 pp., 1937.
103. BRUNINI, REV. JOSEPH BERNARD, J.C.D., The Clerical Obligations of Canons 139 and 142, X-121 pp., 1937.
104. CONNOR, REV. MAURICE, A.B., J.C.D., The Administrative Removal of Pastors, VIII-159 pp., 1937.
105. GUILFOYLE, REV. MERLIN JOSEPH, J.C.D., Custom, XI-144 pp., 1937.
106. HUGHES, REV. JAMES AUSTIN, A.B., A.M., J.C.D., Witnesses in Criminal Trials of Clerics, IX-140 pp., 1937.
107. JANSEN, REV. RAYMOND J., A.B., S.T.L., J.C.D., Canonical Provisions for Catechetical Instruction, VII-153 pp., 1937.
108. KEALY, REV. JOHN JAMES, AB., J.C.D., The Introductory Libellus in Church Court Procedure, XI-121 pp., 1937.
109. MCMANUS, REV. JAMES EDWARD, C.SS.R., J.C.D., The Administration of Temporal Goods in Religious Institutes, XVI-196 pp., 1937.
110. MORIARTY, REV. EUGENE JAMES, J.C.D., Oaths in Ecclesiastical Courts, X-115 pp., 1937.

111. RAINER, REV. ELIGIUS GEORGE, C.SS.R., J.C.D., Suspension of Clerics, XVII-249 pp., 1937.
112. REILLY, REV. THOMAS F., C.SS.R., J.C.D., Visitation of Religious, VI-195 pp., 1938.
113. MORIARTY, REV. FRANCIS E., C.SS.R., J.C.D., The Extraordinary Absolution from Censures, XV-334 pp., 1938.
114. CONNOLLY, REV. NICHOLAS P., J.C.D., The Canonical Erection of Parishes, X-132 pp., 1938.
115. DONOVAN, REV. JAMES JOSEPH, J.C.D., The Pastor's Obligation in Prenuptial Investigation, XII-322 pp., 1938.
116. HARRIGAN, REV. ROBERT J., M.A., S.T.B., J.C.D., The Radical Sanation of Invalid Marriages, VIII-208 pp., 1938.
117. BOFFA, REV. CONRAD HUMBERT, J.C.D., Canonical Provisions for Catholic Schools, VII-211 pp., 1939.
118. PARSONS, REV. ANSCAR JOHN, O.M.Cap., J.C.D., Canonical Elections, XII-236 pp., 1939.
119. REILLY, REV. EDWARD MICHAEL, A.B., J.C.D., The General Norms of Dispensation, XII-156 pp., 1939.
120. RYAN, REV. GERALD ALOYSIUS, A.B., J.C.D., Principles of Episcopal Jurisdiction, XII-172 pp., 1939.
121. BURTON, REV. FRANCIS JAMES, C.S.C., A.B., J.C.D., A Commentary on Canon 1125, X-222 pp., 1940.
122. MIASKIEWICZ, REV. FRANCIS SIGISMUND, J.C.D., Supplied Jurisdiction According to Canon 209, XII-340 pp., 1940.
123. RICE, REV. PATRICK WILLIAM, A.B., J.C.D., Proof of Death in Prenuptial Investigation, VIII-156 pp., 1940.
124. ANGLIN, REV. THOMAS FRANCIS, M.S., J.C.D., The Eucharistic Fast, VIII-183 pp., 1941.
125. COLEMAN, REV. JOHN JEROME, J.C.D., The Minister fo Confirmation, VI-153 pp., 1941.
126. DOWNS, REV. JOSEPH EMMANUEL, A.B., J.C.D., The Concept of Clerical Immunity, XI-163 pp., 1941.
127. ESSWEIN, REV. ANTHONY ALBERT, J.C.D., Extrajudicial Penal Powers of Ecclesiastical Superiors, X-144 pp., 1941.
128. FARRELL, REV. BENJAMIN FRANCIS, M.A., S.T.L., J.C.D., The Rights and Duties of the Local Ordinary Regarding Congregations of Women Religious of Pontifical Approval, V-195 pp., 1941.
129. FEENEY, REV. THOMAS JOHN, A.B., S.T.L., J.C.D., Restitutio in Integrum, VI-169 pp., 1941.
130. FINDLAY, REV. STEPHEN WILLIAM, O.S.B., A.B., J.C.D., Canonical Norms Governing the Deposition and Degradation of Clerics, XVII-279 pp., 1941.
131. GOODWINE, REV. JOHN, A.B., S.T.L., J.C.D., The Right of the Church to Acquire Property, VIII-119 pp., 1941.
132. HESTON, REV. EDWARD LOUIS, C.S.C., Ph.D., S.T.D., J.C.D., The Alienation of Church Property in the United States, XII-222 pp., 1941.

133. HOGAN, REV. JAMES JOHN, A.B., S.T.L., J.C.D., Judicial Advocates and Procurators, XII-200 pp., 1941.
134. KEALY, REV. THOMAS M., A.B., Litt.B., J.C.D., Dowry of Women Religious, IX-152 pp., 1941.
135. KEENE, REV. MICHAEL JAMES, O.S.B., J.C.D., Religious Ordinaries and Canon 198, V-164 pp., 1942.
136. KERIN, REV. CHARLES A., S.S., M.A., S.T.B., J.C.D., The Privation of Christian Burial, XVI-279 pp., 1941.
137. LOUIS, REV. WILLIAM FRANCIS, M.A., J.C.D., Diocesan Archives, X-101 pp., 1941.
138. MCDEVITT, REV. GILBERT JOSEPH, A.B., J.C.D., Legitimacy and Legitimation, X-247 pp., 1941.
139. MCDONOUGH, REV. THOMAS JOSEPH, A.B., J.C.D., Apostolic Administrators, X-217 pp., 1941.
140. MEIER, REV. CARL ANTHONY, A.B., J.C.D., Penal Administration Procedure Against Negligent Pastors, XI-240 pp., 1941.
141. SCHMIDT, REV. JOHN ROGG, A.B., J.C.D., The Principles of Authentic Interpretation in Canon 17 of the Code of Canon Law. XII-331 pp., 1941.
142. SLAFKOSKY, REV. ANDREW LEONARD, A.B., J.C.D., The Canonical Episcopal Visitation of the Diocese, X-197 pp., 1941.
143. SWOBODA, REV. INNOCENT ROBERT, O.F.M., J.C.D., Ignorance in Relation to the Imputability of Delicts, IX-271 pp., 1941.
144. DUBE, REV. ARTHUR JOSEPH, A.B., J.C.D., The General Principles for the Reckoning of Time in Canon Law, VIII-299 pp., 1941.
145. MCBRIDE, REV. JAMES T., A.B., J.C.D., Incardination and Excardination of Seculars, XX-585 pp., 1941.
146. KROL, REV. JOHN T., J.C.D., The Defendant in Ecclesiastical Trials, XII-207 pp., 1942.
147. COMYNS, REV. JOSEPH J., C.SS.R., A.B., J.C.D., Papal and Episcopal Administration of Church Property, XIV-155 pp., 1942.
148. BARRY, REV. GARRETT FRANCIS, O.M.I., J.C.D., Violation of the Cloister, XII-260 pp., 1942.
149. BOLDUC, REV. GATIEN, C.S.V., A.B., S.T.L., J.C.D., Les Études dans les Religions Clericales, VII-155 pp., 1942.
150. BOYLE, REV. DAVID JOHN, M.A., J.C.D., The Juridic Effects of Moral Certitude on Pre-Nuptial Guarantees, XII-188 pp., 1942.
151. CANAVAN, REV. WALTER JOSEPH, M.A., Litt.D., J.C.D., The Profession of Faith, XII-143 pp., 1942.
152. DESROCHERS, REV. BRUNO, A.B., PH.L., S.T.B., J.C.D., Le Premier Concile Plenier de Quebec et le Code de Drôit Canonique, XIV-186 pp., 1942.
153. DILLON, REV. ROBERT EDWARD, A.B., J.C.D., Common Law Marriage, X-148 pp., 1942.
154. DODWELL, REV. EDWARD JOHN, PH.D., S.T.B., J.C.D., The Time and Place for the Celebration of Marriage, X-156 pp., 1942.

155. DONNELLAN, REV. THOMAS ANDREW, A.B., J.C.D., The Obligation of the Missa pro Populo, VII-131 pp., 1942.
156. ELTZ, REV. LOUIS ANTHONY, A.B., J.C.D., Cooperation in Crime, XII-208 pp., 1942.
157. GASS, REV. SYLVESTER FRANCIS, M.A., J.C.D., Ecclesiastical Pensions, XI-206 pp., 1942.
158. GUINIVEN, REV. JOHN JOSEPH, C.SS.R., J.C.D., The Precept of Hearing Mass, XIV-188 pp., 1942.
159. GULCZYNSKI, REV. JOHN THEOPHILUS, J.C.D., The Desecration and Violation of Churches, X-126 pp., 1942.
160. HAMMILL, REV. JOHN LEO, M.A., J.C.D., The Obligations of the Traveler According to Canon 14, VIII-204 pp., 1942.
161. HAYDT, REV. JOHN JOSEPH, A.B., J.C.D., Reserved Benefices, XI-148 pp., 1942.
162. HUSER, REV. ROGER JOHN, O.F.M., A.B., J.C.D., The Crime of Abortion in Canon Law, XII-187 pp., 1942.
163. KEARNEY, REV. FRANCIS PATRICK, A.B., S.T.L., J.C.L., The Principles of Canon 1127.
164. LINAHEN, REV. LEO JAMES, S.T.L., J.C.D., De Absolutione Complicis In Peccato Turpi, 114 pp., 1942.
165. MCCLOSKEY, REV. JOSEPH ALOYSIUS, A.B., J.C.D., The Subject of Ecclesiastical Law According to Canon 12, XVII-246 pp., 1942.
166. O'NEILL, REV. FRANCIS JOSEPH, C.SS.R., J.C.D., The Dismissal of Religious in Temporary Vows, XIII-220 pp., 1942.
167. PRINCE, REV. JOHN EDWARD, A.B., S.T.D., J.C.D., The Diocesan Chancellor, X-136 pp., 1942.
168. RIESNER, REV. ALBERT JOSEPH, C.SS.R., J.C.D., Apostates and Fugitives from Religious Institutes, IX-168 pp., 1942.
169. STENGER, REV. JOSEPH BERNARD, J.C.D., The Mortgaging of Church Property, 186 pp., 1942.
170. WALDRON, REV. JOSEPH FRANCIS, A.B., J.C.D., The Minister fo Baptism, XII-197 pp., 1942.
171. WILLETT, REV. ROBERT ALBERT, J.C.D., The Probative Value of Documents in Ecclestiastical Trials, X-124 pp., 1942.
172. WOEBER, REV. EDWARD MARTIN, M.A., J.C.D., The Interpellations, XII-161 pp., 1942.
173. BENKO, REV. MATTHEW ALOYSIUS, O.S.B., M.A., J.C.D., The Abbot *Nullius*, XIV-148 pp., 1943.
174. CHRIST, REV. JOSEPH JAMES, M.A., S.T.L., J.C.D., Dispensation from Vindicative Penalties, XIV-285 pp., 1943.
175. CLANCY, REV. PATRICK M. J., O.P., A.B., S.T.LR., J.C.D., The Local Religious Superior, X-229 pp., 1943.
176. CLARKE, REV. THOMAS JAMES, J.C.D., Parish Societies, XII-147 pp., 1943.
177. CONNOLLY, REV. JOHN PATRICK, S.T.L., J.C.D., Synodal Examiners and Parish Priest Consultors, X-223 pp., 1943.

178. Drumm, Rev. William Martin, A.B., J.C.D., Hospital Chaplains, XII-175 pp., 1943.
179. Flanagan, Rev. Bernard Joseph, A.B., S.T.L., J.C.D., The Canonical Erection of Religious Houses, X-147 pp., 1943.
180. Kelleher, Rev. Stephen Joseph, A.B., S.T.B., J.C.D., Discussions with non-Catholics: Canonical Legislation, X-93 pp., 1943.
181. Lewis, Rev. Gordian, C.P., J.C.D., Chapters in Religious Institutes, XII-169 pp., 1943.
182. Marx, Rev. Adolph, J.C.D., The Declaration of Nullity of Marriages Contracted Outside the Church, X-151 pp., 1943.
183. Matulenas, Rev. Raymond Anthony, O.S.B., A.B., J.C.L., Communication, a Source of Privileges, XII-225 pp., 1943.
184. O'Leary, Rev. Charles Gerard, C.SS.R., J.C.D., Religious Dismissed After Perpetual Profession, X-213 pp., 1943.
185. Power, Rev. Cornelius Michael, J.C.D.,The Blessing of Cemeteries, XII-231 pp., 1943.
186. Shuhler, Rev. Ralph Vincent, O.S.A., J.C.D., Privileges of Regulars to Absolve and Dispense, XII-195 pp., 1943.
187. Ziolkowski, Rev. Thaddeus Stanislaus, A.B., J.C.D., The Consecration and Blessing of Churches, XII-151 pp., 1943.
188. Heneghan, Rev. John Joseph, S.T.D., J.C.D., The Marriages of Unworthy Catholics: Canons 1065 and 1066, XVI-213 pp., 1944.
189. Carroll, Rev. Coleman Francis, M.A., S.T.L., J.C.L., Charitable Institutions.
190. Ciesluk, Rev. Joseph Edward, Ph.B., S.T.L., J.C.L., National Parishes in the United States.
191. Coburn, Rev. Vincent Paul, A.B., J.C.D., Marriages of Conscience, XII-172 pp., 1944.
192. Connors, Rev. Charles Paul, C.S.Sp., A.B., J.C.L., Extra-Judicial Procurators in the Code of Canon Law, X-94 pp., 1944.
193. Coyle, Rev. Paul Raymond, A.B., J.C.L., Judicial Exceptions.
194. Fair, Rev. Bartholomew Francis, A.B., S.T.L., J.C.L., The Impediment of Abduction.
195. Gallagher, Rev. Thomas Raphael, O.P., A.B., S.T.Lr., J.C.L., The Examination of the Qualities of the Ordinand, X-166 pp., 1944.
196. Gannon, Rev. John Mark, S.T.L., J.C.L., The Interstices Required for the Promotion to Orders, XII-100 pp., 1944.
197. Goldsmith, Rev. J. William, B.C.S., S.T.L., J.C.L., The Competence of Church and State over Marriage—Disputed Points, X-128 pp., 1944.
198. Goodwine, Rev. Joseph Gerard, A.B., S.T.B., J.C.L., The Reception of Converts, XIV-326 pp., 1944.
199. Kowalski, Rev. Romuald Eugene, O.F.M., A.B., J.C.D., Sustenance of Religious Houses of Regulars, X-174 pp., 1944.
200. McCoy, Rev. Alan Edward, O.F.M., J.C.D., Force and Fear in Re-

lation to Delictual Imputability and Penal Responsibility, XII-160 pp., 1944.

201. McDEVITT, REV. VINCENT JOHN, Jh.B., S.T.L., J.C.L., Perjury.
202. MARTIN, REV. THOMAS OWEN, Ph.D., S.T.D., J.C.D., Adverse Possession, Prescription and Limitation of Actions: The Canonical "Praescriptio," XX-208 pp., 1944.
203. MIKLOSOVIC, REV. PAUL JOHN, A.B., J.C.L., Attempted Marriages and Their Consequent Juridic Effects.
204. MUNDY, REV. THOMAS MAURICE, A.B., S.T.L., J.C.L., The Union of Parishes.
205. O'DEA, REV. JOHN COYLE, A.B., J.C.D., The Matrimonial Impediment of Nonage, VIII-126 pp., 1944.
206. OLALIA, REV. ALEXANDER AYSON, S.T.L., J.C.D., A Comparative Study of the Christian Constitution of States and the Constitution of the Philippine Commonwealth, XII, 136 pp., 1944.
207. POISSON, REV. PIERRE-MARIE, C.S.C., A.B., Ph.L., J.C.L., Droits Patrimoniaux des Maisons et des Eglises Religieuses.
208. STADALNIKAS, REV. CASIMIR JOSEPH, M.I.C., J.C.D., Reservation of Censures, X-141 pp., 1944.
209. SULLIVAN, REV. EUGENE HENRY, S.T.L., J.C.D., Proof of the Reception of the Sacraments, X-165, pp., 1944.
210. VAUGHAN, REV. WILLIAM EDWARD, J.C.D., Constitutions for Diocesan Courts, X-210 pp., 1944.
211. PARO, REV. GINO, S.T.D., J.C.L., The Right of Apostolic Delegation.
212. BALZER, REV. RALPH FRANCIS, C.P., J.C.L., The Computation of Time in a Canonical Novitiate.
213. DOUGHERTY, REV. JOHN WHELAN, A.B., S.T.L., J.C.L., De Inquisitione Speciali.
214. DZIOB, REV. MICHAEL WALTER, J.C.L., The Sacred Congregation for the Oriental Church.
215. EIDENSCHINK, REV. JOHN ALBERT, O.S.B., B.A., J.C.L., The Election of Bishops in the Letters of Pope Gregory the Great.
216. GILL, REV. NICHOLAS, C.P., J.C.L., The Spiritual Prefect in Clerical Religious Houses of Study.
217. HYNES, REV. HARRY GERARD, S.T.L., J.C.L., The Privileges of Cardinals.
218. McDEVITT, REV. GERARD VINCENT, S.T.L., J.C.D., The Renunciation of an Ecclesiastical Office, XIV-179 pp., 1945.
219. MANNING, REV. JOSEPH LEROY, J.C.L., The Free Conferral of Offices.
220. MEYER, REV. LOUIS G., O.S.B., A.B., S.T.B., J.C.D., Alms-Gathering by Religious, XII-163 pp., 1945.
221. O'DONNELL, REV. CLETUS FRANCIS, M.A., J.C.L., The Marriage of Minors.
222. PRUNSKIS, REV. JOSEPH, J.C.D., Comparative Law, Ecclesiastical and Civil, in Lithuanian Concordat, X-161, pp., 1945.

223. Sweeney, Rev. Francis Patrick, C.Ss.R., J.C.D., The Reduction of Clerics to the Lay State, X-199 pp., 1945.

224. Vogelpohl, Rev. Henry John, J.C.L., The Simple Impediments to Holy Orders.

225. Brockhaus, Rev. Thomas G., O.S.B., J.C.L., Religious Who Are Known as Conversi.

226. Griese, Rev. N. Orville, S.T.D., J.C.L., Marriage and Procreation of Offspring.

227. Boudreaux, Rev. Warren Louis, J.C.L., The "ab acatholicis nati" of Canon 1099, 2.

228. Bowe, Rev. Thomas Joseph, A.B., J.C.L., Religious Superioresses.

229. Diederichs, Rev. Michael Ferdinand, S.C.J., J.C.L., The Jurisdiction of the Latin Ordinaries over their Oriental Subjects.

230. Dingman, Rev. Maurice John, A.B., S.T.L., J.C.L., The Plaintiff in Contentious Trials.

231. Frison, Rev. Basil M., C.M.F., M. Mus., J.C.L., The Retroactivity of Law.

232. Galvin, Rev. William Anthony, M.A., J.C.L., The Administrative Transfer of Pastors.

233. Goracy, Rev. Joseph C., J.C.L., The Diriment Matrimonial Impediment of Major Orders.

234. Hale, Rev. Joseph Francis, M.A., S.T.L., J.C.L., The Pastor of Burial.

235. Henry, Rev. Joseph, A.B., J.C.L., The Mass and Holy Communion: Interritual Law.

236. Linenberger, Rev. Herbert, C.PP.S., J.C.L., Falsa Delatio (Can. 893 and 2363).

237. Lowry, Rev. James Martin, B.A., J.C.L., Dispensation from Private Vows.

238. Lynch, Rev. George Edward, A.B., S.T.L., J.C.L., Coadjutors and Auxiliaries of Bishops.

239. Lynch, Rev. Timothy, M. S. SS. T., J.C.L., Contracts Between Bishops and Religious Congregations.

240. McClunn, Rev. Justin David, A.B., S.T.L., J.C.L., Administrative Recourse.

241. McGarvey, Rev. Thomas Joseph, A.B., S.T.L., J.C.L., Bination.

242. McGrath, Rev. James, A.B., J.C.L., The Privilege of the Canon.

243. Marbach, Rev. Joseph Francis, A.B., J.C.L., Marriage Legislation for the Catholics of the Oriental Rites in the United States and Canada.

244. Shimkus, Rev. Bernard Aloysius, A.B., J.C.L., The Determination and Transfer of Rite.

245. Smith, Rev. Vincent M., S.T.L., J.C.L., Ignorance Affecting Matrimonial Consent.

246. Wachtrle, Rev. Paul Anthony, A.B., J.C.L., The Baptism of the Children of Non-Catholics.

www.ingramcontent.com/pod-product-compliance
Lightning Source LLC
LaVergne TN
LVHW050212080826
844660LV00012B/399

* 9 7 8 0 8 1 3 2 2 4 2 0 6 *